# Adult Literacy, Numeracy and Language

# Adult Literacy, Numeracy and Language: Policy, Practice and Research

*edited by*
*Lyn Tett, Mary Hamilton and Yvonne Hillier*

Open University Press
Maidenhead   New York

Open University Press
McGraw-Hill Education
McGraw-Hill House
Shoppenhangers Road
Maidenhead
Berkshire
England
:L6 2QL

email: enquiries@openup.co.uk
world wide web: www.openup.co.uk

and Two Penn Plaza, New York, NY 10121-2289, USA

First published 2006

Copyright © Lyn Tett, Mary Hamilton and Yvonne Hillier

A catalogue record of this book is available from the British Library

ISBN-10:  0 335 21937 3 (pb) 0 335 21938 1 (hb)
ISBN-13:  978 0335 21937 7 (pb)  978 0335 21938 4 (hb)

Library of Congress Cataloguing-in-Publication Data
CIP data applied for

Typeset by BookEns Ltd, Royston, Herts.
Printed in Poland by OZ Graf. S.A.
www.polskabook.pl

# Contents

## Section Three: The Politics of Numbers

## Section Four: Measuring and Assessing Adult Literacy, Numeracy and Language

## Section Five: Crossing Boundaries: Facilitating Interactions

# Foreword

It was my good fortune to participate as discussant in the first ESRC seminar on social practices approaches to adult basic education, held at Lancaster University in October of 2002. The focus of the seminar series and of this book is on the application of the social practices framework to issues in adult basic skills education. Social practices approaches have long offered us a vital and promising theoretical framework for understanding the basic skills of adults in richer and more productive ways – whether literacy, numeracy or oral language. Despite the impressive theoretical advances of the social practices framework, often called 'new literacy studies', relatively little progress has been made in applying the framework to practical problems of policy and programme design in adult education and training. That gap is greatly reduced by this current, important volume.

The social practices perspective has grown out of, and in reaction to, an older and narrower psychological approach that focuses only on individual cognitive skills. The social practices approach helps us think about what it is that people know and do in everyday life, and helps to locate *meanings, values* and *purposes* within a basic skills framework. The book argues that literacy, numeracy and language are more than a set of skills or techniques; they are cultural practices shaped by the social and historical contexts in which they occur and by the meanings they have and the purposes they serve for their participants. This approach shifts the focus from narrowly functional and externally imposed definitions of literacy, numeracy, communication and language to more open and numerous definitions that focus on what people do with their basic skills, with whom, when and how.

The book considers a rich variety of ways in which social practice approaches may be applied to key issues of policy and programme implementation in the United Kingdom and further afield. These issues are addressed within the current policy climate in which literacy, numeracy and language are the subject of great interest for governments. As I read the chapters, several points I raised in my commentaries at the seminar have re-emerged, points that illustrate the rich ways in which new literacy studies can inform and reshape adult basic skills education in many countries. One point is about *assessment*, another is about *standards-driven systemic reform,* and the third is about the notion of a *literacy problem.*

Many problematic tensions between the social practices framework and the predominant assessment methods used for adult basic skills are identified in this volume. Less clear is how adult basic skills assessments should be changed to fit a social practices framework. In this regard, it may be helpful to consider the difference between the social practices conception of *doing a literacy practice skilfully* and the functional skills conception of *having a literacy skill.* The central difficulty in the functional skills conception can be illustrated by the 'dipstick' metaphor of automobiles and petrol. Individuals walk around with so much literacy ('petrol') in their heads; they are assessed by opening up their heads and inserting 'dipsticks'; all too often they are 'down a quart' and need to be 'filled up'. The social practices view, by way of contrast, is more concerned with the literacy practices that people actually perform in everyday life and the skilfulness with which they perform those literacy practices.

The social practices view clearly affords a more nuanced and textured framework in which to assess adults' basic skills. The proponents of the social practices approach – many of whom have contributed to this volume – have offered repeated (and, in my mind, persuasive) critiques of the standardized functional skills-based assessments of adult literacy, numeracy and language. As vitriolic as the ensuing debates have become, there has been little movement to develop a practical alternative assessment scheme. Can we not apply the social practices approach to develop more meaningful and informative surveys of literacy practices in our populations? The work of Victoria Purcell-Gates and colleagues (see, for instance, the *Development of Print Literacy*, Harvard University Press, 2004) illustrates how the measurement of literacy practices can illuminate adults' literacy development. Although there are many conceptual and technical challenges to be addressed, it is surely time for such efforts to move forward. And as we think more carefully about assessment, we must examine not only the instruments and methodologies being utilized, but also the *assessment practices* and the contexts, purposes and meanings they carry for the learners and others involved in their implementation. We need to examine who is affected by these practices, in what ways, and who benefits from these practices. Deborah Brand, in *Literacy in American Lives* (Cambridge University Press, 2001), has suggested that literacy practices are often influenced by remote 'sponsors', that is, by temporally or spatially distant persons or institutions. We should not be surprised to find remote 'sponsors' for various assessment practices as well.

Beyond inviting us to reconsider the assessment of adults' basic skills, the social practices approach also challenges us to think more deeply about the provision of adult basic skills education more generally. Once we recognize the essentially inseparable nature of social context and literacy, the social practices of the many actors involved in provision become centrally important. The book nicely illustrates how adult basic skills provision can be understood as a system of interacting social practices. Not only are the student's observed literacy practices critical, so are the instructors'. The social practices of programme directors, curriculum developers, and teacher trainers are all of considerable interest in this regard. Special attention should be paid to the central importance of various *standards* in the systemic reform of adult education. The *Skills for Life* strategy currently being implemented in England is an example of *standards-driven systemic reform* in adult education. The book considers various aspects of this systemic reform from the social practices perspective.

The social practices framework can also help us better understand the crucial notion of *others'* demands for adults' basic skills to increase. Critiques of large-scale assessments such as the International Adult Literacy Survey (IALS) – critiques found in this volume and elsewhere – often note the disjuncture between literacy 'problems' identified through surveys of test scores and those reported directly by survey participants. Such surveys regularly find that many more adults score below some externally defined testing benchmark than report having difficulties in everyday life with specific literacy tasks. This disjuncture is sometimes taken as evidence that the underlying skills assessment cannot be valid. Although this *may* be the case, I draw a different and, I would hope, more generative conclusion from such findings. These findings highlight quite different ways of conceptualizing a 'literacy problem'. When governments or educational agencies report 'problems' related to large numbers of individuals having 'substandard' basic skills, we should ask for whom it is a problem, or more succinctly, whose problem it is. Is it a problem for the assessed person (remember the dipstick)? Or is it a problem for the educational agency? For employers? Society? The more of this volume I read, the more I came to believe that a 'literacy problem' is often best defined as a *difference in expectations* regarding the performance of literacy or numeracy practices. So, for example, when learners score poorly in relation to a national strategy such as Skills for Life, yet fail to report difficulties performing everyday tasks drawing on those same skills, the real *problem* may well be the discrepant perceptions about literacy or numeracy.

Given a richer construct of 'literacy problems', we may be better able to develop new ways of addressing them. We may not always be limited to strategies of just 'filling them up' with basic skills training. We may also be able to develop programmes that help resolve literacy problems through the innovative use of assistive technologies, or through collaborations of individuals of varying literacy and numeracy abilities, or by devising other contextual supports to facilitate basic skills development.

Although this book raises these and many other important and interesting issues, it does not resolve all of them. This is entirely as it should be. Much progress is described in applying the social practices approach to important questions of policy and programme design for adult basic skills. I think you will be excited by the progress you will read about, and challenged to join the authors and others in thinking further about the work remaining to be done.

Stephen Reder
Portland State University
USA
2005

# Contributors

**Elsa Auerbach** is a Professor of English at the University of Massachusetts, Boston. She has worked in factories, community and union-based ESOL programmes, community colleges and university contexts, always attempting to link education with social justice and community action. Her research and publications focus on participatory research and curriculum development.

**David Barton** is Director of the Literacy Research Centre at Lancaster University. Current interests include: literacy and social justice; the relation between adult learners' lives and their participation in learning; the changing nature of literacy in contemporary society. A recent co-edited book on learning is *Beyond Communities of Practice* (Cambridge University Press, 2005).

**Mark Baxter** became a teacher/researcher while teaching numeracy in a prison. He taught and worked in fine art for many years, after training and work in the electrical engineering industry. An interest in teaching measurement and its relation to teaching numeracy led him to join the measurement group. He now teaches in FE colleges in South London.

A sociolinguist by training and applied linguist by affiliation, **Mike Baynham** has worked in England and Australia where he was Director of the Centre for Language and Literacy at the University of Technology, Sydney. His research interests currently include: academic literacies, adult ESOL; narrative and migration. He is currently Professor of TESOL at the University of Leeds.

**Diana Coben** is Reader in Adult Numeracy at King's College London and has published widely in this developing field. She was Founding Chair of Adults Learning Mathematics (www.alm-online.org), an international research forum and a founder member of the National Research and Development Centre for Adult Literacy and Numeracy (www.nrdc.org.uk).

**Jay Derrick** has worked since 1975 as a teacher and manager in adult literacy, numeracy and language, in the voluntary sector, for LEAs and for FE colleges. Since 2003 he has been an independent consultant, focusing mainly on evaluation, research and project management in teacher training development, workplace learning and assessment.

**Harvey Goldstein** is Professor of Social Statistics at Bristol University – a part-time post-retirement position. There are two main foci of his research. The first is the use of statistical modelling techniques in the construction and analysis of educational tests. The second is in the methodology of multilevel modelling. The major text on multilevel modelling is his book *Multilevel Statistical Models* Edward Arnold, 2003).

**Mary Hamilton** is Professor of Adult Learning and Literacy in the Department of Educational Research at Lancaster University and Associate Director of the Literacy Research Centre. She coordinates the NRDC's Practitioner-Led Research Initiative and is course director for Lancaster's online learning master's programme in adult literacy, numeracy and ESOL (www.lancs.ac.uk/depts/edres/study/diploma/diploma.htm).

**Yvonne Hillier** is Professor of Postcompulsory Education at City University. She has taught across the education sector including special education, adult basic skills, tutor training and postgraduate programmes, examining the policy and practice of adult learning. She recently completed an ESRC-funded project with Mary Hamilton (University of Lancaster) on the history of adult basic skills.

**Ursula Howard** has worked in adult literacy, numeracy and language since 1974 as a teacher, organizer, manager and more recently as a director of national research and development projects. She is currently preparing for publication her own research on the acquisition and meaning of learning to write in 19th-century England.

**Peter Lavender** is Deputy Director of NIACE and coordinator of research and development. Before this he was a further education funding council inspector in the basic education area. He has served on bodies concerned with adult education, basic skills and disability, including UNESCO and the Moser Technical Implementation Group. He chairs the committee on disability at the LSC.

**Eamonn Leddy** has worked with adults and numeracy for over 20 years in Inner London. He started as a volunteer and part timer in adult education and has worked in a number of FE colleges since the mid-1990s. His involvement in the 'Measures Project' for the NRDC was his first involvement in research as a practitioner.

**Juliet Merrifield** is Principal of the Friends Centre, an independent adult education centre in Brighton. She has worked as an adult educator and researcher for the last 25 years, both in the USA and England. She was Director of the Learning from Experience Trust in London, and of the Center for Literacy Studies at the University of Tennessee, USA.

**Mary Norton** is co-coordinator and facilitator at The Learning Centre, a community-based adult literacy and education centre in

Edmonton, Alberta, Canada. Her work with adult learners at the centre provides touchstones for her research in practice and facilitation of professional development workshops and courses.

After nearly 30 years working in the computer industry, **Liz Richards** changed direction and now teaches numeracy in a large Inner London FE college.

**Celia Roberts** is Senior Research Fellow in the Department of Education and Professional Studies at King's College London. Her publications in the fields of urban discourse, second language socialization and intercultural communication include: *Talk, Work and Institutional Order* (Mouton, 1999, with Sarangi) and *Language Learners as Ethnographers* (Multilingual Matters, 2000, with Byram et al.).

**Lyn Tett** is Professor of Community Education at the University of Edinburgh. She has been involved in ALNE since 1977, initially as a practitioner, then as a policy advisor and developer and currently as a researcher. She is particularly interested in the discourses of social exclusion that surround current policy initiatives.

**Alison Tomlin** worked in adult and community education for about 25 years, and then moved to research. Her work as a tutor and organizer includes literacy, numeracy and community education; her work in research includes developing research projects collaboratively with students and supporting practitioner research projects in numeracy.

**Mahendra Verma** has taught, researched and published in the areas of language maintenance, shift and death, language policies and ideology in education, adult and child bilingualism and biliteracy in the context of the South Asian ethnic minority communities in the UK. More recently he has been researching on the impact of globalization and English on languages in India.

Prior to joining the teaching profession, **Topo Wresniwiro** worked in industry for over 13 years. He had also taught maths in schools in London for seven years before switching to adult education. Topo became involved in the 'Measures Project' for the NRDC as teacher-researcher while teaching maths in a high-security prison in Southeast London.

# Dedication

This book is dedicated to the memory of Claire Catherine Mary Jones, Lyn's much loved daughter-in-law, who died on 15 October 2005, aged 40. Claire was a mathematician and computer scientist whose pleasure in conveying the power and joy of numbers to friends, colleagues and family will be sadly missed.

## Acknowledgements

Our thanks are due to the Economic and Social Research Council (R451265195) for funding the seminar series on which this book is based and to the NRDC and Scottish Executive, which provided additional funding to enable greater numbers of practitioners to participate. We are particularly grateful to the many participants in the series who made the dialogue between practitioners, policymakers and researchers so productive in enabling us all to learn and share during the series and to continue these dialogues through this book. Important contributors to this process were the administrative staff, Pam Holgate and Viv Edwards at Edinburgh, Kathryn James at Lancaster, Karen Small and Jas Kaur at City, who all remained calm in the face of potential disasters and efficiently steered this project home. Finally, a big thank you to our families and our students for supporting us during the seminars and in the production of this book.

# Abbreviations

**ACAL** Australian Council for Adult Literacy
**ACER** Australian Council for Educational Research
**ALBSU** Adult Literacy and Basic Skills Unit
**ALLP** Australian Language and Literacy Policy
**ALN** adult literacy and numeracy
**ALNE** adult literacy and numeracy and ESOL
**ALNL** adult literacy, numeracy and language
**ANCC** adult numeracy core curriculum
**AoC** Association of Colleges
**BBC** British Broadcasting Corporation
**BSA** Basic Skills Agency
**CALC** Community Adult Learning Council
**CALP** Community Adult Learning Programme
**CEC** Commission of the European Communities
**CITO** Centraal Instituut voor Toetsontwikkeling
**CLS** Center for Literacies Studies
**DEET** Department for Education and Employment
**DES** Department of Education and Science
**DES/WO** Department of Education and Science/Welsh Office
**DfEE** Department for Education and Employment
**DfES** Department for Education and Skills
**DIY** do it yourself
**EdExcel** Educational Excellence
**EFA** Education For All
**EFL** English as a foreign language
**ERSC** Economic and Social Research Council
**ESL** English as a second language
**ESOL** English for speakers of other languages; English as a second or other language
**EU** European Union
**FE** further education
**FTI** Fast Track Initiative
**GATS** General Agreement on Trade in Services
**GCSE** General Certificate of Secondary Education
**GED** general equivalency diploma

**HMSO** Her Majesty's Stationery Office
**IAG** information, advice and guidance
**IALS** International Adult Literacy Survey
**ICT** information and communications technology
**ILP** individual learning plan
**IMF** International Monetary Fund
**LLN** literacy, language and numeracy
**LLU+** Language and Literacy Unit Plus
**LSC** Learning and Skills Council
**LSDA** Learning Skills Development Agency
**NAEP** national assessment of educational progress
**NCSALL** National Center for the Study of Adult Learning and Literacy
**NFER** National Foundation for Educational Research
**NIACE** National Institute of Adult Continuing Education
**NLS** new literacy studies
**NGO** nongovernmental organization
**NHS** National Health Service
**NLS** National Literacy Secretariat
**NQF** National Qualifications Framework
**NRDC** National Research and Development Centre
**ODPM** Office of the Deputy Prime Minister
**OECD** Organization for Economic Cooperation and Development
**PAR** participatory action research
**PISA** Programme for International Student Assessment
**PSA** public sector agreement
**QCA** Qualifications and Curriculum Authority
**RAE** research assessment exercise
**RaPAL** research and practice in adult literacy
**RCT** randomized controlled trials
**SLA** second language acquisition
**SLS** second language socialization
**UCLES** University of Cambridge Local Examinations Syndicate
**UNESCO** United Nations Educational, Scientific, and Cultural Organization
**UTS** University of Technology, Sydney
**VTALP** Volunteer Tutor Adult Literacy Programme

# 1 Introduction: Social Practice of Adult Literacy, Numeracy and Language

*Mary Hamilton, Yvonne Hillier and Lyn Tett*

## Why read this book and why it matters

The topic of basic communication skills – literacy, numeracy and language – has long been of central concern within education and training. Its importance is felt across a wide range of educational contexts. Longstanding debates about how best to teach and organize these skills have been increasingly unsettled by the changing communication technologies through which we learn and carry out our day-to-day lives. This book focuses on adult learners and on contemporary understandings about how they can access adult literacy, numeracy and language (ALNL) in post-school contexts. This focus reflects the expertise of the authors and the high topicality of adult lifelong learning within policy across the UK and in many other countries.

The book takes as its starting point a reconceptualization of these basic communication tools that has gradually been happening over the last 20 years as part of a bigger paradigm shift in our understanding of learning as part of situated social practice. The specific approach has been called the 'new literacy studies' and is actually a cluster of closely related theories that have moved away from a traditional psychological or cognitive skills model to one that includes the social practices associated with number, reading and writing. It is a social view rather than a purely psychological one. It sees literacy and numeracy as being historically and socially situated and therefore part of cultural and media theory. Brian Street describes this as a shift from seeing literacy as an autonomous gift to be given to people, to an ideological understanding of literacy that places it in the wider context of institutional purposes and power relationships (see Street 1995).

This reconceptualization is what led the editors to establish a seminar series, funded by the ESRC, where leading policymakers, practitioners and researchers from the UK, Europe and North America debated how a social practice view of ALNL can develop and inform policy and practice. The seminar participants met together and continued their discussions over a two-year period resulting in a rich dialogue that contributes to our understanding of how the ALNL field is constructed. We asked: how useful is this theory and the evidence it offers of the diversity of literacies and numeracies in everyday lives? How might it enhance our understanding of what we are doing in the educational field of adult language, literacy, numeracy and therefore the strategies that are used within policy and practice?

This book is the first attempt to elaborate these ideas, based on a dialogue between people working as researchers, policymakers and practitioners in the countries of the United Kingdom. The point of bringing practitioners, researchers and policy actors together is that each group has developed its own ways of talking about ALNL. Dialogue enables us to explore the kinds of translation that might be made between them. Is it possible for academic theories to be translated into useful insights for effective teaching and learning? How can practitioner knowledge guide policy actions? What are the obstacles to this happening?

We believe that the chapters in this book demonstrate convincingly that the social practices view of adult literacy, numeracy and language is indeed a good and practical theory, which offers us quite a different perspective from the 'functional skills' approach and one which can guide us as we move into exciting new areas of practice and policy.

## The social practice approach and how it contrasts with the functional skills approach

In this section we want to explain what we mean by a social practice approach to literacy, language and numeracy and the alternative position with which it is often contrasted, a 'functional skills' approach.

Our argument is that ALNL are part of social practices that are observable in 'events' or 'moments' and are patterned by social institutions and power relationships. This encourages us to look beyond texts themselves to what people *do* with literacy, numeracy and language, with whom, where, and how. That is, we focus attention on the cultural practices within which written and spoken words and numbers are embedded – the ways in which texts are socially regulated and used and the historical contexts from which these practices have developed. This leads us to consider the differentiated uses of ALNL in varying cultural contexts and in the mass media including visual and oral ways of communicating (see Kress and Van Leeuwen 1996). It directs attention to the interlinking uses of these different media, both old (print) and new (electronic) technologies. Not just reading, but also speaking and writing become central to the definition of literacy and other ways of interacting with print culture are also identified.

This view of ALNL demands that we make connections: with the community in which learners lead their lives outside the classroom; with a notion of situated learning; between learning and institutional power; between print literacy and other media; between our own literacies as teachers and researchers, users and the theory presented here. By contrast a 'functional skills-based' approach focuses attention on the autonomy of the text and the meanings it carries. It searches for universal features of adult literacy, numeracy and language and other semiotic sign systems. It leads to narrow, reductionist definitions of reading, writing and calculating and ignores aspects of learning that cannot be dealt with at the psychological or cognitive level. In this way, we maintain that it excludes many issues that are important for understanding learner responses. By the same token, the focus of the social practices approach shifts from ALNL as deficit or lack, something people have not got, to the many different ways that people engage with ALNL, recognizing difference and diversity and challenging how these differences are valued within our society.

There is not just one 'social practices theory' of adult literacy, numeracy and language but a number of different versions. The social practice approach that has characterized the 'new literacy studies' (NLS) draws mainly on ideas and methodologies from sociology, socio-linguistics and anthropology that can be distinguished from the more psychological approach of socio-historical activity theory, rooted in the ideas of Lev Vygotsky and others. A review paper by Glenda Hull and Kathryn Schultz (2001) is useful in clarifying these different theoretical roots and positions for those who are interested in taking this up. Stephen Reder's paper on 'practice engagement theory' is also a good resource for seeing how the Vygotskian approach might be applied to ALNL (Reder 1994).

The NLS involves us in looking beyond educational settings to informal learning, and to the other official settings in which literacies play a key role. Learning does not just take place in classrooms and is not just concerned with methods. As Steve Reder commented at the first seminar, the social practices perspective helps us think about what it is that people know and do in everyday life, and helps to locate *meanings*, *values* and *purposes* within a broader literacy framework, not simply looking at the texts themselves.

How far might it be possible (or desirable) to reconcile the two approaches – the functional skills approach and the social practices approach – within policy and practice? Are they mutually exclusive alternatives, entirely different ways of conceiving of literacy and numeracy, or are they compatible? For example, could we conceive of the social practices approach as *encompassing* and extending the narrower focus of 'skills'? If we see 'skills' in this way as just one part of socio-cultural practice then how can we develop the theory better to show this integration? To date, the Vygotskian socio-cultural approach (see Daniels 2001) has worked out better answers to this than the new literacy studies, partly because it has focused more directly on pedagogical settings where the terminology of skills is frequently used, whereas the new literacy studies has been deliberately looking at everyday cultural settings that are harder to pin down in terms of organized learning.

The idea of two opposing broad approaches (social practice versus skills) is of course an oversimplification and there are other ways of characterizing the guiding philosophies people have brought to ALNL (Cobb 1994; Hamilton 1996). A more nuanced discussion is offered by, for example, Peter Freebody and Joseph Lo Bianco in *Australian Literacies* where they set out some practical ideas about what a national policy on literacy should say (Freebody and Lo Bianco 1997). They distinguish between three families of thought about literacy, derived from a survey of Australian literacy teachers. They call these (1) skill, (2) personal growth and heritage approaches and (3) critical–cultural approaches. The personal growth and heritage approach is typified by Richard Hoggart in his classic book *The Uses of Literacy* (Hoggart 1957). The critical approach has developed from the work of the Brazilian educator Paulo Freire (Freire 1973) and includes writers such as Colin Lankshear and Elsa Auerbach (Auerbach 1992; Lankshear 1997). They also add a challenge to these approaches from the recent 'multiliteracies' approach described in Cope and Kalantzis (2000).

Freebody and Lo Bianco then go on to distinguish between a range of approaches to teaching and learning: literature-based, natural learning, experience-based learning, skills-based, genre-based and cultural prac-tice-based approaches. These are related to the families of thought above, although not necessarily in a one-to-one way. Trying to draw the best from all of these, they suggest (see Freebody and Lo Bianco 1997: 26) that effective literacy tuition draws on a repertoire of resources that allow learners to:

- break the code
- participate in the meanings of text
- use texts functionally
- analyse texts critically.

The terms and conclusions that Freebody and Lo Bianco discuss are not identical to those we might identify in the UK context. However, their deliberations are an important example of an attempt to relate theory, practice and policy, especially as Joseph Lo Bianco was a main architect of the Australian National Language and Literacy policy in the 1980s and early 1990s.

The point of raising these distinctions is to show that in designing a policy, important choices have to be made that privilege certain approaches over others and to suggest that these choices may have implications at the micro level of teaching and learning. Unlike the Australian context, where the theoretical understandings on which choices were made were explicitly discussed, in the UK there has been no such discussion, at least not in any public forum. This leaves the impression that there are no alternative ways of approaching literacy and numeracy, that policy strategies are simply 'technical, best value' solutions rather than choices motivated by ways of thinking about the nature of adult literacy, numeracy and language. The briefest glance at what is known about the policy process, however, reveals that part of the power of policy is to stabilize the meanings associated with a social issue, through its choice of discourses – that policy itself constructs the problem it intends to address (see Ball 1990; Lo Bianco and Wickert 2001; Moore 2002).

A main aim of this book, then, is to bring to the surface the assumptions that lie beneath current policy and practice so that we can question them in relation to issues that we claim to be important, such as supporting and encouraging diversity, social inclusion and equality of access to literacy and numeracy. This book is an invitation to readers to map out their own position in relation to these approaches as a basis for engaging in debate about these issues.

## Current contexts of adult language, literacy and numeracy learning in England and Scotland

In their chapter about policy context in *Powerful Literacies*, written in 2001, Hamilton, Tett and Macrae (2001) sketched the history of developments in adult literacy, numeracy and language in the four countries of the UK. They wrote optimistically about the possibilities for embedding a social practice approach in what was then a rapidly changing field called adult basic education:

> This is a moment of opportunity for ABE in the UK ... in which we can build on our history of participatory approaches to adult learning, the strong tradition of voluntary associations, and new research which can underpin and justify a broadly based and

sustainable approach to practice. (Hamilton, Tett and Macrae 2001: 39)

They pointed out how individual countries can exert a strong national steer over policy and practice but this will inevitably be within a wider framework of interconnected social polices and international agendas. They identified both the continuities and differences between provision in the four countries of the UK and the pull towards conformity in current systems:

> Despite the histories of each country which reveal diverse approaches to literacy and the organization of ABE, the dominance of the English educational and policy frameworks both structurally and ideologically are evident across the UK. ABE in England is still the most systematized and narrowly defined first and foremost as part of education or training (rather than a social or community development issue). This vision also drives mainstream developments in Northern Ireland and Wales and is in contrast to the community development approach which has figured most strongly in Scotland and the EU funded projects in Northern Ireland targeted at improved conditions within the religious communities ... As the present international pressures come to bear on the field more strongly, the impulse toward conformity will increase. The contrary trend of devolution of political power to individual countries and regions is the main assurance against this happening and the future shape of ABE will be one test of the robustness of the autonomy that has been achieved. (Hamilton, Tett and Macrae 2001: 37)

Since 2001 the situation has improved and ALNL has achieved more secure funding and an institutional base in the UK. The publication of the International Adult Literacy Survey 'league tables' for international literacy and numeracy rates played a major role in the drive to increase participation rates in the adult population, but also fuelled a deficit view of people's existing capabilities (see Hamilton and Barton 2000). The policy agenda emphasizes basic literacy and numeracy, lifelong learning and the use of new communications technologies. It views these as crucial to developing basic/core/key competences as a foundation for economic prosperity in a knowledge economy. Although these themes permeate provision in the four countries of the UK, we are now going to discuss how current policy and practice in England and Scotland are oriented to the different approaches to ALNL outlined in the previous section.

## Commodification of literacy and numeracy: SMART targets and a high stakes culture in England

Since coming to power in 1997, the New Labour government has strongly supported the development of basic skills, both in schools through the National Literacy and Numeracy Strategies and among adults through the Skills for Life strategy. This support is both rhetorical and financial. Talk of lifelong learning prevalent in the late 1990s has dropped away, although a rationale of social inclusion is still used (Department for Education and Employment 1998; Fryer 1997; Moser 1999; Tomlinson 1996). The shape of ALNL is increasingly justified in relation to vocational goals. Standardization of the field has intensified along with quality controls and accountability to funders. There is a strong emphasis on standardized tests and learner qualifications that fit with the national vocational qualification system and will follow seamlessly from the key skills now embedded within initial education. Because of the way in which funding has been targeted, participation is increasingly skewed towards younger adults, those with less complex learning needs and those with a lesser distance to travel toward the achievement targets (Bathmaker 2005).

There are now separate core curricula for ESOL, literacy and numeracy, new national qualifications, a baseline national literacy test and a system of professional training for teachers, based on standards and new qualifications. Widely publicized national targets drive an expanded service with heavy promotion of computer-based learning technologies for both teacher training and learner provision and the use of local partnerships between different agencies. All this is under the control of a new funding agency, the Learning and Skills Council that dispenses funding across the post-compulsory sector.

Despite the rhetoric of social inclusion and citizen participation, the present system is driven by a market ideology and a vision of the needs of global economic competitiveness: creating a skilled workforce and an active consumer, rather than an informed citizen. It is based on a top-down definition of literacy where need is defined for learners rather than negotiated with them on the basis of their perceived needs. However subtle and flexibly designed the curriculum is, it cannot transcend this fundamental feature: it is designed *for* learners rather than *with* them or *by* them. To this extent, the more open and humanistic possibilities of a lifelong (and lifewide) system of learning opportunities for literacy and numeracy are weakened and obscured. For practitioners, the tightly drawn boundaries around their work throw up new tensions as they attempt to deal with the messy reality of diverse learning needs and settings while 'ticking the right boxes'.

## Curriculum framework for adult literacy and numeracy in Scotland

Scotland has taken longer to develop a national curriculum partly because the body responsible for developing adult literacy numeracy and language, Communities Scotland: Learning Connections, was not established until early in 2002. The other reason for the slower development was that the group charged with developing the curriculum framework built in three consultations with ALNL practitioners and managers and so the process took nearly two and a half years with the curriculum being published in May 2005 (Scottish Executive 2005). A curriculum for ESOL is still in the process of development at the time of writing (autumn 2005). The Scottish approach has been to develop a learner-centred framework, rather than a specified content, for its ALN curriculum. The emphasis is on the way that the curriculum is negotiated with learners and builds creatively on their existing knowledge and skills. It is built around the four contexts of private, family, community and working lives that reflect the importance of the learner's real life and everyday practices. It specifically espouses a social practices approach to the curriculum and assessment is based on 'distance travelled' (Scottish Executive 2005: 22) rather than standardized tests.

This different approach reflects the Scottish educational context that has always had a stronger consultative approach to curriculum initiatives than England (see Paterson 2003), partly because there is a much smaller community of practice and so has been more open to responding to practitioners' views. The Scottish ALNL field has also been predominately community based and so has had a more learner focused approach to learning and assessment that have at their heart the aim of improving access and quality within the context of a consultative and empowering policy process (Scottish Executive 2001).

There are, however, some problematic issues raised by the openness of the approaches to learning, teaching and assessment. The first of these is the lack of clear guidance on what should be available to be learned and taught and this demands a great deal of the tutor in negotiating a suitable curriculum with each individual learner. This is particularly difficult in the context of a teaching workforce that is predominantly part time or unpaid. Another problematic area is the approach to assessment, which is based on an individual learning plan, as this is time consuming and again is overly reliant on the professional expertise of the tutor to implement it effectively. The third problematic area is that training for tutors is still not fully developed and so the necessary expertise to deliver the curriculum is not yet in place. Finally, funding is based on numbers of learners participating in tuition and, although this avoids some of the problems associated with standardized tests, it does mean that there can be an emphasis on the more easy to recruit learners rather than the hardest to reach, such as young people.

## Implications of a social practice view of literacy, language and numeracy for educational practice, policy and research

What difference does a theory make to learners and to teaching practice? Does it result in people doing things any differently? There are a few existing examples of policy and practice being based on this approach, of which current literacies policy in Scotland, as outlined above is a key example. A recent book edited by Brian Street (*Literacies across Educational Contexts*, 2005) is the first collection to bring together such examples ranging from early years to adult education in a range of international settings. The examples in this book emphasize two important principles underlying the implementation of a social practice approach to literacy, numeracy and language:

1   A two-way dialogue and movement is essential between formal learning and the everyday world. Everyday, situated cultures and practices cannot be simply acknowledged and imported into classroom settings. The boundaries between 'in' and 'out' of education must be blurred such that contexts become permeable. Formal learning practices and educators themselves move out of classrooms into the everyday world, and in the process will themselves be transformed.
2   A process of active, expansive learning is assumed by this approach. It characterizes the process of becoming numerate or literate as one of 'taking hold of' the tools of number and language. This has important implications for relationships in the learning process and the room in the curriculum for reflective and questioning activity on the part of both learners and teachers (as described by Hamilton 2000). By extension, the ways in which both teachers and learners participate in decision making and the governance of the organization in which learning takes place, through management committees, consultative bodies, research and development activities, are crucial. Citizenship is modelled and enacted within such arenas.

The implications for practice are not just in terms of the curriculum and the teaching and learning process itself, but the theory of literacy and numeracy as social practice orients us to other significant aspects of provision including the roles of curriculum managers and other key programme personnel often overlooked in research and policy. This helps us broaden and advance our thinking about pedagogy, from a transmission model to a broader process of facilitation and support of learning.

Perhaps the greatest practical contribution of this approach lies in its ability to provide an integrated framework in which the provision of ALNL programmes can itself be understood as a set of literacy practices. This is the focus of the new study of 'academic literacies' and it also offers a way of exploring the power relations involved in institutional practices. The social practice approach allows us to make connections and to ask questions that would be 'out of range' of the functional skills approach. The chapters in this volume demonstrate just how useful such a framework can be for understanding and ultimately improving the design of both programmes and policies.

For example, it reorients us from the purely pedagogical aspects of practice to the imposed systems of performance measurement which are currently a highly significant influence on practitioner work. These shape practitioner experience, attitudes to the job and activities, as indeed they are intended to do, albeit not necessarily *in the ways* that they do. A growing literature on the 'learning organization' and audit culture is helpful in thinking about performance indicators (see Merrifield, forthcoming). The use of performance indicators are a good example of how policy 'disciplines' the field of practice, attempting to shape it within a particular view of what literacy (and pedagogical practice) ideally should be. These requirements also have unintended effects as people react to the demanding and messy day-to-day realities of filing returns, filling in individual learning plans with students, or mustering evidence about achievement within busy schedules. Impossible demands almost set people up to subvert them.

Assessment practices, in particular, have been identified as being very important. These include the ways that progress and achievement are recorded and published and the feedback that is given to students. During the seminar series, participants distinguished between 'outputs' and 'outcomes' and noted that only certain outcomes are measured and valued. Perceptions of learner need are clearly related to the social practice account. If the metaphor of the 'dipstick' approach to measuring literacy, seems to characterize the 'skills' approach to literacy, what would an alternative (or additional?) approach to assessment be, from the point of view of a social approach to adult literacy, numeracy and language?

A social practice account frames the issues of adult literacy, numeracy and language as part of communicative practices. It explains why these diverse subject specialisms are yoked together in policy as 'basic' or 'essential' skills. It enables us to deal with new communication technologies under the same umbrella. It encourages us to identify the similarities between these different technologies as well as their differences.

While adult literacy, numeracy and language skills are distinct specialisms, all three are fundamental aspects of communication that both mediate individuals' dealings with one another, and regulate interaction with social agencies. This gives rise to questions about the different value and attention paid to the different areas. For example, why has there been a consistent lack of practitioner skills and attention to numeracy? Why do all groups (providers, policymakers, general public) collude with the fact that it is acceptable not to be good with numbers despite the evident high status of numerical evidence in society as a whole and research that demonstrates that numeracy does make a difference to adult life chances? What is this all about?

It is a further step to think through the implications *for policy* of a social practice approach to adult literacy, numeracy and language. Focusing on the social practices of provision as described above, allows us to examine how they are shaped by and respond to policy. Gaps do exist in the meanings, ideas and discourses that circulate within policy domains/practice and theory. There are contradictions in policy that can be explored and exploited by practice. Such contradictions can result, for example, in a clash of funding mechanisms. However, a policy strategy does not necessarily dictate pedagogy – the relationship is not deterministic. Policy tends to simplify in its effort to stabilize meaning and practitioners have to avoid being trapped by this. Practitioners encounter, and have to work with, complexity and particularly have to focus on the learner as adult.

Historical roots run deeply in the field of adult literacy, numeracy and language. The cultural politics identified with theorists like Raymond Williams and social historians like Jane Mace and David Vincent (Mace 1992; Vincent 1993; Williams 1989) are still highly relevant in unpicking the dynamics of change and agency in the field. Is change made by nameless (or infamous!) policymakers from on high? Do practitioners make change? Do learners? Where, in our systems of authorship, representation and discussion does any exchange of ideas happen between these three groups, how do new ideas circulate and take root in systematic ways? What kind of 'intermediaries' might help this process? One of the strengths of the social practice approach to literacy is that it enables us to encompass and address such questions rather than limiting us to micro-level issues of teaching and learning methods in the here and now: what kinds of model do we have of how to influence policy? Beneath these assumptions, what notions do we hold of 'civil society'? Is policy 'citizen responsive' or is it imposed from above? This connection to theories of citizenship is an important one that is taken forward in this book.

Finally, the social practices approach to adult literacy, numeracy and language has implications for research. It sees research as itself part of the social practices it investigates and questions the boundaries of authority and the traditional power hierarchies built into the research, practice and policy communities. Whose knowledge is considered legitimate in the field? What remains invisible or devalued? Through its emphasis on a reflexive practice, it advocates breaking down these barriers, for example by practitioners engaging in research activities, policymakers and researchers respecting the diversity of everyday lived knowledge of learners and practitioners so that this can be built into the systems that are developed. The development of public spaces where evidence, values and theory can be deliberated across the traditional divides is at the heart of this approach.

In summary, the social practices approach might change policy, practice and research through its emphasis on:

- the diversity of learners, learning preferences and expression through different technologies and how to explore and bring that into policy and educational practice in the classroom
- seeing literacy, numeracy and language as more than individual skills, they are communal resources, integral to the social interactions, relationships and institutions within which they are used and developed
- the everyday uses and activities of ALNL, what these mean to people, and the implication that academic/educational pedagogic practice is one among many specialized contexts in which ALNL is encountered – so enabling connected analysis of these
- blurring the boundaries between, in, and out of, education thereby revealing how deeply literacies and numeracies are embedded in everyday life purposes (a different logic to the pedagogic one) and in social relationships that vary across the different institutional contexts that give them their meaning
- the power of discourses in framing and shaping understandings of the field and therefore the importance of developing new vocabularies for talking about languages, literacies and numeracies, and of linking existing discourses in new ways
- the long view: analysing change and the historical roots of educational policy, practice and technological means of realizing learning

- new aspects of the teaching and learning process, including the role of performance indicators as specialized working practices, their effects on teachers and learners and the central role of adult literacy, numeracy and language themselves as tools in the audit process
- encouraging a reflexive and questioning stance that enables/ supports mutual exploration of adult literacy, numeracy and language using ethnographic methods and practitioner enquiry. In this sense it encourages critical enquiry. It is not just meant to be descriptive but engaged – it changes the situation it analyses by articulating new understandings and learners and teachers to actively 'take hold' of adult literacy, numeracy and language and shape it for their own purposes.

## How can this book be used?

One of our key aims in producing this book has been to go on building networks so that the dialogue between researchers, policymakers and practitioners started during the seminars can continue. We hope that the book will act as a focal point for participants on professional development courses, and those involved more broadly in policy and research, to enable them to enter the debates started in these pages. To this end we have organized the chapters into five sections, each dealing with a different theme and each presenting perspectives from policy, practice and research.

Section One, *Literacies as Situated Social Practice*, highlights and explains the differences between the social practice and functional skills approaches to literacies provision. David Barton gives an overview, from a research perspective, of the social practice view of literacy through a focus on the things people do in their lives that demonstrates the situated nature of literacies. Ursula Howard shows how this approach can positively inform policies through demonstrating its practical value for attaining government's economic and social inclusion targets in more effective ways than the 'skills model'. In the concluding chapter in this section, Lyn Tett focuses on practice, research and policy in Scotland and the impact of their three-way interrelationship, to examine how the social practices approach can contribute to social inclusion.

In Section Two, *Literacy, Language and Multilingualism*, Elsa Auerbach, Celia Roberts and Mahendra Verma explore literacy events and practices in the lives of bilingual learners, bilingualism and biliteracy in a literacy-dominated western urban culture and society and the separation of race/ ethnicity issues, cultural processes and language. The social practices paradigm is interrogated and unpacked and its functions examined in the light of broader questions of power and social change in order to see how research, policy and practice can make a difference in learners' lives. A case study is provided of the literacy practices of a minority ethnic community and the implications of multilingualism. Auerbach focuses on the potential for social practices research, in alliance with critical theories of literacy, to shift traditional power relations, deepen analysis of issues from the social contexts of participants' lives and lead toward action. Roberts focuses on policy in second language acquisition and the need for an overarching framework that incorporates the wider social context of inequality and explicitly recognizes bi/multilingual resources in building capacity, and developing provision. Verma focuses on the literacy practices and literary events in South Asian communities with reference to one vibrant and dynamic literacy and oracy event but shows the impact that the the lack of commitment in the UK to bi/multiliteracy has on younger generations.

Section Three, *The Politics of Numbers*, applies the social practice perspective to numeracy. The authors consider the social context in which people's actions, including their mathematical actions and interpretations of information involving mathematics, have meaning, based on a view of the human being as a social being and of mathematics as human activity. Mike Baynham explores the number-saturated social world into which we are all born and the power and politics of naming as ways of knowing the world. He suggests that numbers can position us as subjects but also enable us by giving us another kind of tool for thinking with. He focuses on the social practices perspective on numeracy research in a variety of settings in order to explore the power and possibility of numbers. Diana Coben focuses on socio-cultural approaches to adult numeracy and mathematics education and learning and discusses the differences between a social practices view of literacies and that of numeracy. She argues that adult numeracy education policy is at last moving to the mainstream but wonders if a socio-cultural approach will necessarily relieve us of the obsession with skills at the expense of knowledge and understanding. The final chapter in this section is by four teacher–researchers and a researcher who worked together on a numeracy project that focused on measurement. Mark Baxter, Eamonn Leddy, Liz Richards, Alison Tomlin and Topo Wresni- wiro discuss the problems of doing research as practitioners and what this means for learners in the under-researched and under-valued area of adult numeracy. They show how the recognition of cultural diversity and the multiplicity of knowledges brought to solving and under- standing mathematical problems are consistent with a social practices approach.

Section Four is entitled *Measuring and Assessing Adult Literacy, Numeracy and Language*. In it, Harvey Goldstein, examines the implementation of the 'Education For All' declaration by UNESCO to explore the influence of the International Adult Literacy Survey and its effect on practice in a range of developed and developing countries. He shows the impact of how we measure basic skills, and the methodological issues this raises, through a focus on the distortions caused by 'high-stakes' testing, and demonstrates how reliance on the achievement of numerical 'targets' reveals undesirable side effects and distorts educational systems. Two case studies of the effect of government targets and national tests in relation to the national 'adult basic skills strategy' in England from Peter Lavender and Jay Derrick show how the best of intentions can lead to disaster. Lavender focuses on an analysis of policies in England and shows how the strong link between tests, qualifications and funding can exclude particular learners and particular provision. He suggests that the national (English) tests will not widen participation because they are an inflexible way of measuring individual progress and of encouraging more people to participate. Derrick focuses on performance measurement in the FE sector in England that he characterizes as the 'command and control' approach to quality improvement and shows how it impacts adversely at both the institutional level and on teaching practice. He puts forward an alternative model that uses a 'complex systems' approach to reform educational assessment that would include a much wider range of assessment methods and tools and the use of descriptive, narrative and qualitative discourses as well as quantitative and numerical data.

In the fifth and final section, *Crossing Boundaries: Facilitating Interactions*, three writers – Juliet Merrifield, Mary Norton and Yvonne Hillier – describe their experiences of the back and forth of boundary crossings. They show how they moved between the three domains of research, policy and practice, across sectors within education and training, across countries in the UK and across continents. All three explore the tensions inherent in applying a social practice of ALNL by interrogating the strengths and weaknesses of the theory with a focus on ensuring that learning opportunities are available to all that will make a difference to people's lives in ways that are positive and empowering. Merrifield focuses on exploring the boundary crossing of practice, policy and research through the ideas of popular knowledge, literacy learning as a tool to change lives and the relationships between research, practice and policies and shows that boundaries are more permeable and messier than we might think. Norton focuses on policy, research and practice within the particular context of a community literacy programme in Canada and explores the issues raised for social learning, power and participation for social practices theory. Hillier interrogates the claims made by the social practices approach for policy and practice by exploring the claims made in the numerous contexts of this book. She also shows how the boundaries between research, policy and practice need to be crossed backwards and, more importantly, forwards through taking the notion of critical reflection and action research to inform our practice.

# References

Auerbach, E. (1992) *Making Meaning, Making Change: Participatory Curriculum Development for Adult ESL/Literacy.* Washington, DC: Center for Applied Linguistics, Delta Publications.

Ball, S. (1990) *Politics and Policy Making.* London: Routledge.

Barton, D. and Hamilton, M. (1998) *Local Literacies: A Study of Reading and Writing in One Community.* London: Routledge.

Barton, D., Hamilton, M. and Ivanic, R. (eds) (2000) *Situated Literacies.* London: Routledge.

Bathmaker, A. (2005) *Achieving the adult basic skills targets in England: what picture can we gain from available statistical data and what issues does this raise?* Unpublished paper presented to BERA Conference, Pontpridd, September.

Cobb, P. (1994) 'Where is the mind? Constructivist and sociocultural perspectives on mathematical development'. *Educational Researcher,* 23(7): 13–20.

Cope, B. and Kalantzis, M. (2000) *Multi-literacies: Literacy Learning and the Design of Social Futures.* London: Routledge.

Crowther, J., Hamilton, M. and Tett, L. (eds) (2001) *Powerful Literacies.* Leicester: NIACE.

Daniels, H. (2001) *Vygotsky and Pedagogy.* London: RoutledgeFalmer.

Department for Education and Employment (1998) *The Learning Age: A Renaissance for a New Britain.* London: The Stationery Office.

Freebody, P. and Lo Bianco, J. (1997) *Australian Literacies Part II: What a National Policy on Literacy Should Say.* Canberra: Language Australia.

Freire, P. (1973) *Pedagogy of the Oppressed.* New York: Seabury Press.

Fryer, R. (1997) *Learning for the Twenty-First Century: First Report of the National Advisory Group for Continuing Education and Lifelong Learning (NAGCELL1. PP62/3111634/1297/33).* London: Government Stationery Office.

Hamilton, M. (1996) in Fieldhouse, R. (ed.) *A History of Modern Adult Education.* Leicester: NIACE.

Hamilton, M. (2000) 'Ethnography for the classroom'. Special Issue of the *Journal of Curriculum Studies* (renamed *Pedagogy, Culture and Society*) on *Literacy in the Curriculum*, 7(3): 429–44.

Hamilton, M. (2002) 'Sustainable literacies and the ecology of lifelong learning'. Position paper for the Open University/University of East London Global Colloquium on Supporting Lifelong Learning, 5–7 July 2000, and published in Harrison, R., Reeve, F., Hanson, A. and Clarke, J. (eds) *Supporting Lifelong Learning Volume 1: Perspectives on Learning*. Milton Keynes: Routledge/Open University Press.

Hamilton, M. (2005) 'Understanding the everyday: adult lives, literacies and informal learning' in McKeough, A., Phillips, L., Timmons, V. and Lupart, J. (eds) *Understanding Literacy Development: A Global View*. Newark, NJ: Lawrence Erlbaum Associates Inc.

Hamilton, M. and Barton, D. (2000) 'The International Literacy Survey: what does it measure?'. *International Journal of Education*, Hamburg: UNESCO.

Hamilton, M., Barton, D. and Ivanic, R. (eds) (1994) *Worlds of Literacy*. Clevedon: Multilingual Matters.

Hamilton, M., Tett, L. and Macrae, C. (2001) *Powerful Literacies: The Police Context* in Crowther, J., Hamilton, M. and Tett, L. (eds) *Powerful Literacies*. Leicester: NIACE.

Hoggart, R. (1957) *The Uses of Literacy: Aspects of Working-class Life with Special Reference to Publications and Entertainment*. London: Chatto & Windus.

Hull, G. and Schultz, K (2001) 'Literacy and learning out of school: a review of theory and research'. *Review of Educational Research*, 71(4): 575–611.

Kress, G. and van Leeuwen, T. (1996) *Reading Images: The Grammar of Visual Design*. London: Routledge.

Lankshear, C. (1997) *Changing Literacies*. Milton Keynes: Open University Press.

Lavender, P., Derrick, J. and Brooks, B. (2004) *Testing, Testing, 123*. Leicester: NIACE.

Lo Bianco, J. and Wickert, R. (eds) (2001) *Language and Literacy Policy in Australia: 30 Years of Action*. Melbourne: Language Australia.

Mace, J. (1992) *Talking About Literacy*. London: Routledge.

Macrae, C. (2000) *Literacies in the Community: Resources for Practitioners and Managers*. Edinburgh: Scottish Office.

Merrifield, J. (forthcoming) *Accountability in Skills for Life Learning*. London: NRDC Report.

Moore, H. (2002) 'Who will guard the guardians themselves? National interest versus factional corruption in policymaking for ESL in Australia' in Tollefson, J. (ed.) *Language Policies in Education*. New York: Lawrence Erlbaum Associates Inc.

Moser, C. (1999) *A Fresh Start: Improving Literacy and Numeracy*. London: Department for Education and Employment.
Paterson, L. (2003) *Scottish Education in the Twentieth Century*. Edinburgh: Edinburgh University Press.
Reder, S. (1994) 'A sociocultural approach to literacy across language and cultures' in Ferdman, B., Weber, R-M. and Ramirez, A.G. (eds) *Literacy Across Languages and Cultures*. New York: State University of New York Press.
Scottish Executive (2001) *Literacy and Numeracy in Scotland*. Edinburgh: The Stationery Office.
Scottish Executive (2005) *A Curriculum Framework for Adult Literacy and Numeracy for Scotland*. Edinburgh: Learning Connections, Communities Scotland.
Street, B. (1995) *Social Literacies: Critical Approaches to Literacy in Development, Ethnography and Education*. London: Longman.
Street, B. (ed.) (2005) *Literacies Across Educational Context: Mediating Learning and Teaching*. Philadelphia, PA: Caslon Publishing.
Tomlinson, S. (1996) *Inclusive Learning: Report of the Learning Difficulties and/or Disabilities Committee*. London: The Stationery Office.
Vincent, D. (1993) *Literacy and Popular Culture: England 1750–1914*. Cambridge: Cambridge University Press.
Williams, R. (1989) *What I Came to Say*. London: Hutchinson Radius.

## Useful websites

Juliet Merrifield's 'Contested ground: performance accountability in adult basic education' can be downloaded from The US National Centre for Studies in Adult Learning and Literacy (NCSALL) at www.ncsall.gse.harvard.edu under Research Reports #1. Many other useful downloadable publications can be found here too.
Mary Hamilton's paper on 'Sustainable literacies and the ecology of life-long learning' is downloadable at www.open.ac.uk/lifelonglearning/papers/index.html.
The AILA virtual forum pages at www.education.leeds.ac.uk/AILA/VirtSem1 contain a paper by Peter Freebody (Griffith University, Australia), 'Assessment as communal versus punitive practice: six new literacy crises'. Responses by Brian Street (Kings, London) and Cathy Kell (University of Cape Town, South Africa).

# Section One
## Literacies as Situated Social Practice

# 2 Significance of a Social Practice View of Language, Literacy and Numeracy

*David Barton*

Language, literacy and numeracy are central to knowledge and communication. Fundamental social and technological changes affecting our lives mean that the nature of knowledge and the nature of communication are changing. For instance, the internet is changing what we know and how we find things out, who we communicate with and how. What we mean by literacy and numeracy and being literate or numerate is changing and researchers across a range of disciplines are asking basic questions about the nature and significance of literacy and numeracy. Within the study of literacy this work can be loosely drawn together in what is becoming known as a social practice theory. This provides a coherent framework for thinking about literacy which has implications in all areas of education and which is being taken up and applied to learning in different contexts. This is also true in the more general study of language and to a lesser extent in the study of numeracy (as in Diana Coben's chapter in this volume).

In this chapter, I provide an overview of this social view of literacy, drawing the wide range of research in different settings which has now been done. In particular I will draw on examples from the study of people's everyday uses of reading and writing which we carried out in Lancaster, reported in the book *Local Literacies* (Barton and Hamilton 1998), and the studies reported in the book *Situated Literacies* (Barton, Hamilton and Ivanic 2000). These studies were specifically of literacy; I see close parallels in the study of language as a social practice and of numeracy as a social practice in the ways in which language, literacy and numeracy are intertwined in everyday life. They are all part of the symbolic resources and the communicative resources we draw on in life. I return to this issue at the end of this chapter.

This overview is based on Chapter 1 of *Situated Literacies*, in which Mary Hamilton and I presented the theory of literacy as social practice in the form of a set of six propositions about the nature of literacy. These are given in the box that follows. Each of the propositions is useful when thinking about adults and education, whether it is in the context of literacy, language, numeracy, diversity, social inclusion, or international settings. The starting point of this approach is the assertion that *literacy is a social practice*, and the propositions are an elaboration of this. The idea of *literacy practices* offers a powerful way of conceptualizing the link between the activities of reading and writing and the social structures in which they are embedded and which they help shape. When we talk about practices, then, this is not just the superficial choice of a word but the possibilities that this perspective offers for talking about literacy in a useful way and in a way which challenges the dominant skills discourse. For me, the central point is that when literacy is talked about in terms of skills, the 'problem' or 'difficulty' is located in the individual people, who are described as having some kind of deficit. A social practice view of literacy accepts that the situation is more complex than that and problems or difficulties are not just to do with people's failings: issues of debt, or needing help with a form, or not being able to navigate a website raise issues about the complexity of contemporary life as much as attributes of individual people.

---

**Literacy as social practice**

1 Literacy is best understood as a set of social practices; these can be inferred from events mediated by written texts.
2 There are different literacies associated with different domains of life.
3 Literacy practices are patterned by social institutions and power relationships, and some literacies are more dominant, visible and influential than others.
4 Literacy practices are purposeful and embedded in broader social goals and cultural practices.
5 Literacy is historically situated.
6 Literacy practices change and new ones are frequently acquired through processes of informal learning and sense making.

---

To explain this approach in more detail, literacy practices are the general cultural ways of utilizing written language that people draw on in their lives. In the simplest sense, literacy practices are what people *do with literacy*. However, practices are not observable units of behaviour since they also involve values, attitudes, feelings and social relationships. This includes people's awareness of literacy, constructions of literacy and discourses of literacy, how people talk about and make sense of literacy. These are processes internal to the individual; at the same time, practices are the social processes that connect people with one another, and they include shared cognitions represented in ideologies and social identities.

Practices are shaped by social rules that regulate the use and distribution of texts, prescribing who may produce and have access to them. They straddle the distinction between individual and social worlds. Literacy is more usefully understood as existing in the relations between people, within groups and communities, rather than as a set of properties residing in individuals. I provide examples of these points below.

Put simply, the starting point is the things people do in their lives, ranging from routine household activities and leisure activities through to political participation, working and pursuing education. In this approach, we take everyday activities and ask what is the role of reading, writing and texts in the activities. A crucial point which immediately becomes apparent when we look at a range of everyday activities is that most activities in contemporary life involve literacy in some way: we live in a *textually mediated world* and literacy is a central part of participating in most social activities. The way into researching this is through the concept of *literacy events*. Literacy events are activities where literacy has a role. Many literacy events in life are regular, repeated activities, such as paying bills, sending greetings cards, reading bedtime stories; and such activities can often be a useful starting point for practical research into literacy. Some events are linked into routine sequences and these may be part of the formal procedures and expectations of social institutions like workplaces, schools and welfare agencies. Some events are structured by the more informal expectations and pressures of the home or peer group. Events are observable episodes which arise from practices and are shaped by them. The notion of events stresses the situated nature of literacy, that it always exists in a social context.

Usually there is a written text, or texts, central to a literacy event and there may be talk around the text. Texts may be a focal point of the event or they may exist in the background. Texts include rapidly scribbled notes, calendars, books, web pages, text messages, signs, instruction leaflets; there is an almost limitless list of possible text types. In whatever form they appear and however they are used, texts are a crucial part of literacy events and often they provide some stability to activities and across different settings. How such texts are produced and used is a central part of the study of literacy. Literacy education entails learning to produce and use texts, including being able to contribute to texts, and being able to find them, evaluate them and criticize them. Literacy education is about engaging with texts appropriately across a range of settings.

These three components, practices, events and texts, provide the first proposition of a social theory of literacy, that *literacy is best understood as a set of social practices; these can be inferred from events mediated by written texts*. The local literacies study was concerned with identifying the events and texts in people's everyday lives and describing their associated practices. Our prime interest there was to analyse events in order to learn about practices. As with the definition of practices, we take a straightforward view of events at this point, as being activities which involve written texts. An example of an everyday literacy event, taken from the local literacies study, is that of following a recipe when cooking a pudding. It is a simple example where one can imagine a straightforward text, a recipe, and how it might be used. I will use this example to illustrate various points about literacy below.

Once one begins to think in terms of literacy events there are certain things about the nature of reading and writing that become apparent. For instance, in many literacy events there is a mixture of written and spoken language. Many studies of literacy practices have print literacy and written texts as their starting point, but it is clear that in literacy events people use written language in an integrated way as part of a range of symbolic resources and communicative resources; these resources include mathematical systems, graphics, maps and other non-text based images. The cookery text has numeracy mixed with print literacy and the recipes come from books, magazines, the internet, television, as well as orally from friends and relatives. By identifying literacy as one of a range of communicative resources available to members of a community, we can examine some of the ways in which it is located in relation to other mass media and new technologies. What we see is that in the events of everyday life, language, literacy and numeracy, the themes of this book, are integrated and intertwined phenomena. This provides a challenge for language, literacy and numeracy education, where they tend to be thought of as separate: they tend to be taught separately and, in England at least, they have separate curricula and are taught by separate specialists.

Looking more closely at different literacy events, it becomes clear that literacy is not the same in all contexts; rather, there are different *literacies*. The notion of there being different literacies has proved very useful and has been used by people in several senses: for example, practices which involve different media or symbolic systems, such as a film or computer, can be regarded as different literacies, as in *film literacy* and *computer literacy* (along with the more metaphorical *emotional literacy* and *political literacy*). Another sense is that practices in different cultures and languages can be regarded as different literacies, often involving different writing systems (as in Arabic literacy or Chinese literacy). While accepting these senses of the term, the main way in which we use the notion here is to say that literacies are coherent configurations of literacy practices within a culture; often these sets of practices are identifiable and named, as in *academic literacy*, or rather *academic literacies*, and *workplace literacies* and they are associated with particular aspects of cultural life. Within education, literacy has a special role in that it is distinct in different curriculum areas, so that learning to be a cook involves learning to read and write like a cook, learning the literacies of cooking. And these are distinct from the literacies of being a geographer, a nurse, a plumber or a journalist. In addition, literacy is important to teaching and learning itself; education has its own ways of doing things and there are specific *literacies for learning* (and literacies for assessment and literacies for accountability in education). Literacy is central to both what is taught and the way in which it is taught.

Identifying specific educational literacies or workplace literacies means that, within a given culture, *there are different literacies associated with different domains of life*. Contemporary life can be analysed in a simple way into domains of activity, such as home, education, workplace. It is a useful starting point to examine the distinct practices in these domains, and then to compare, for example, home and school, or school and workplace. In our research, we began with the home domain and with everyday life. The home is often identified as a primary domain in people's literacy lives and is central to people's developing sense of social identity. Work is another identifiable domain, where relationships and resources are often structured quite differently from in the home. We might expect the practices associated with cooking, for example, to be quite different in the home and in the workplace – supported, learned and carried out in different ways. The division of labour is different in institutional kitchens, the scale of the operations, the clothing people wear when cooking, the health and safety precautions they are required to take, and so on. These distinct practices in different places can lead to distinct discourse communities or communities of practice. Education can also be seen as a distinct domain and the ways in which cooking is taught within education will, again, be a set of distinct practices, although drawing on and over-lapping with both home and work.

Within these domains there are various institutions that support and structure activities. These include family, religion and government. Some of these institutions are more formally structured than others, with explicit rules for procedures, documentation and legal penalties for infringement, while others are regulated more by the pressure of social conventions and attitudes. Particular literacies have been created by and are structured and sustained by such institutions. However, these domains, and the discourse communities associated with them, are not in any way clear cut: there is a great deal of overlap between domains and there are questions of the permeability of boundaries, of leakages and movement between boundaries. The home domain, for instance, can be located in a broader community domain and education certainly draws on home practices and at the same time shapes and influences home practices. Different subcultures vary in how close their literacy practices are to educational practices and the relationship between home and education is changing. A crucial question for education is what happens to practices as they move across domains.

Socially powerful institutions, such as education, tend to support dominant literacy practices. These dominant practices can be seen as part of whole discourse formations, institutionalized configurations of power and knowledge that are embodied in social relationships. Other vernacular literacies that exist in people's everyday lives are less visible and less supported. This means that *literacy practices are patterned by social institutions and power relationships, and some literacies are more dominant, visible and influential than others*. One can contrast dominant literacies and vernacular literacies; much of the local literacies work has been concerned with documenting the vernacular literacies which exist, and with exploring their relationship to more dominant literacies. Education is about acquiring a broader range of literacies including learning to participate in dominant practices.

People are active in what they do and *literacy practices are purposeful and embedded in broader social goals and cultural practices*. While some reading and writing is carried out as an end in itself, typically literacy is a means to some other end. Any study of literacy practices must therefore situate reading and writing activities in these broader contexts and motivations for use. In the cooking example, for instance, the aim may be to bake a lemon pie, and the reading of a recipe is incidental to this aim. The recipe is incorporated into a broader set of domestic social practices associated with providing food and caring for children or guests, and it reflects broader social relationships and gendered divisions of labour.

A first step in reconceptualizing literacy is to accept the multiple functions literacy may serve in a given activity: it can replace spoken language, enable communication, solve a practical problem or act as a memory aid – in some cases, all at the same time. It is also possible to explore the further work which literacy can do in an activity, and the social meanings it takes on. Literacy has a cognitive aspect, a social aspect and an affective, or emotional, aspect. Texts can have multiple roles in an activity and literacy can act in different ways for the different participants in a literacy event; people can be incorporated into the literacy practices of others without reading or writing a single word. These are all important issues when discussing problems adults have with reading and writing. We almost want to get away from the words *reading* and *writing* and need a new word meaning *dealing with texts*. With shifts to a range of technologies, it is hard to put clear limits on how we define reading and writing.

Another important development is the shift from a conception of literacy located in individuals to examining ways in which people in groups utilize literacy. In this way literacy becomes a community resource, rather than a property of individuals. This is true at various levels; at the detailed micro level, it can refer to the fact that in particular literacy events there are often several participants taking on different roles. At a broader macro level, it can mean the ways in which whole communities use literacy, such as a minority community using writing to assert their identity and to understand their history. There are social rules about who can produce and use particular literacies and it is crucial to understand how texts are regulated socially. Shifting away from literacy as just an individual attribute is one of the most important implications of a practice account of literacy, and one of the ways in which this framework differs most from more traditional accounts. The ways in which literacy acts as a resource for different sorts of groups is a central theme of studies such as the local literacies research, which describe some of the ways in which families, local communities and organizations regulate and are regulated by literacy practices.

Literacy practices are culturally constructed, and, like all cultural phenomena, they have their roots in the past. To understand contemporary literacy it is necessary to document the ways in which *literacy is historically situated*: literacy practices are as fluid, dynamic and changing as the lives and societies of which they are a part. We need a historical approach for an understanding of the ideology, culture and traditions on which current practices are based. The influences of more than 100 years of compulsory schooling in Britain, or several centuries of organized religion, can be identified in the same way as influences from the past decade can be identified. Education today is facing particular challenges, at a time when the practices of schooling which were designed more than a century ago face contemporary social and technological change.

A person's practices are also located in their own history of literacy and adults coming to classes in language, literacy and numeracy bring with them a history of experiences of education which can both help and hinder their participation in learning. In order to understand this we need to take a life history approach, taking account of history within a person's life. The notion of change is central to this: people use literacy to make changes in their lives; literacy changes people and people find themselves in the contemporary world of changing literacy practices. The literacy practices an individual engages with change across their lifetime, as a result of changing demands, available resources, as well as the possibilities and their interests.

Lastly, related to the constructed nature of literacy, any theory of literacy implies a theory of learning. *Literacy practices change and new ones are frequently acquired through processes of informal learning and sense making* as well as formal education and training. This learning takes place in particular social contexts and part of this learning is the internalization of social processes. It is therefore important to understand the nature of informal and vernacular learning strategies and the nature of situated cognition. There needs to be greater dialogue between learning in informal contexts and learning in educational provision. For instance, what are the principles of learning underlying successful learning on youth art projects or in computer gaming? Such issues raise questions about how classroom learning can build on everyday knowledge. In addition, it is necessary to draw on people's insights into how they learn, their theories about literacy and education, the everyday strategies they use to learn new literacies. People's understanding of literacy is an important aspect of their learning, and people's theories guide their actions. It is here that a study of literacy practices has its most immediate links with education and can be the starting point for the development of a social practice theory of literacy pedagogy.

People are doing all sorts of things in their lives, whether it is baking a cake, paying some bills, or surfing the internet, and in doing these things people draw on language, literacy and numeracy. The framework outlined above for literacy can be applied equally well to language and to numeracy. First, language itself is part of most social activities. It is especially important in education to understand that there are different forms or genres of language appropriate to different contexts, and to realize that some forms of language are more valued in some contexts than others. Much advanced study of any subject is learning about the specialized genres appropriate to specific aspects of life. And, as with literacy, there is an interplay between what is learned informally about language and what is taught in formal contexts.

With numeracy there has been some hesitation in viewing this area as a social practice because of the concreteness of the field of knowledge at the centre of numeracy, topics such as counting, measuring and calculation. (See Diana Coben's chapter in this volume.) Nevertheless, if we start from what people do in their everyday lives, it quickly becomes clear that numeracy is a set of social practices. In the local literacies research we saw how numeracy was a frequent and important component of everyday life. Numeracy was integrated with a whole range of symbolic resources in activities as diverse as gardening, health, house repairs, astrology, sports, travelling, shopping. (See Barton and Hamilton 1998: 176–82 for further details.) We also noted that in almost every area in which numbers are used, we could identify more than one system of units, whether we were looking at measurement of distance, of volume, of temperature or of time. People often used more than one system and difficulties were often associated with change and with learning new systems.

The framework outlined above for literacy applies equally to numeracy and it is worth reading through the discussion of literacy above, replacing the word 'literacy' with the word 'numeracy'. This works for most of the discussion: focusing on specific events in order to understand the numeracy practices underlying them is a good starting point; there are different constellations of numeracy used in different domains of life; different forms of numeracy are valued differently and informal learning is a central part of the way people learn new practices. The crucial point for numeracy education which came from our study of everyday life is that when people talked of having difficulties with numbers, it was not necessarily the maths, the calculating, which was the central problem; rather, the maths was located in more general practices. The difficulties were task specific, so that the problems with a gas bill, for example, was a problem with layout, with locating information, with identifying what is important, with understanding the specialized language and with other aspects of meaning making. Here, as with the other examples, the language and literacy associated with numeracy were part of the issue.

Finally, to return to the point made at the very beginning of this chapter, complex and rapid social and technological changes raise fundamental questions about the nature of teaching and learning and the future of formal education. Current forms of educational provision do not fit with the future and we need to return to basic questions about what kind of citizens we want our education system to produce. We need new curricula and new pedagogies. Education for children and adults needs to take account of the fact that everyday learning is often more interesting, more immediate, more fun, better designed and quicker than learning in educational institutions. We live in times when young people are more knowledgeable and skilful in some areas than their teachers and their parents. This raises challenges about what should be taught, how it should be taught and where it should be taught. The challenge is to provide curricula that are designs for the future and that combine skills, creativity, critique and participation to help prepare creative, responsive and active citizens. Education for young people and adults also needs to address issues of equity, access and social justice if they are to be encouraged to participate actively in the future. We then need new pedagogies that address the gap between teaching and learning and that harness new technologies in combination with print technologies.

## References

Barton, D. and Hamilton, M. (1998) *Local Literacies: Reading and Writing in One Community*. London: Routledge.

Barton, D., Hamilton, M. and Ivanic, R. (eds) (2000) *Situated Literacies*. London: Routledge.

## 3 How Could a Socio-cultural Approach to Literacy, Language and Numeracy Inform Policy?

*Ursula Howard*

### Introduction

This chapter uses the concept of socio-cultural approaches to literacy, language and numeracy (LLN), building on David Barton's definition and exploration of social practice in the previous chapter. I look at how such an approach can positively inform the development of policies that focus on the learning of literacy beyond school. I use a particular view of culture as 'ordinary' in the sense of 'a way of life' (Williams 1981) and thus closely related to social practice, in order to emphasize issues of inequality in access to educational and cultural resources, including literacy and numeracy. Inequality and social division are perpetuated in policy decision making and strategies, despite some real gains in recent years in the UK in policies on poverty, early years education and potentially adult LLN. Raymond Williams, Pierre Bourdieu and others have argued powerfully that the ability and means to use literacy is still based on social class (Bourdieu 1993; Williams 1961; Williams 1984). This is borne out by recent UK government research, which shows that access to literacy and numeracy is still determined by social class: people from social class 5 were roughly four times more likely to have literacy problems than those in social class 1, as measured by the ability to reach level 2 in the current national test in England (DfES 2003). Literacy and its expression as social practice remain exclusive. Barriers block the visibility of literacy, and the wider ways of life, of many people, who are in effect culturally excluded. Using socio-cultural approaches to inform policy could help to effect change.

### The 'skills model'

Dominant forms of publicly funded LLN learning since the 1980s have focused on the skills of individuals and their use value to the economy. Further, the criticism levelled at the skills model of LLN is that it is predicated on skills and wider attributes which are judged lacking in individuals, who are then seen as inadequate as people. It is a 'deficit' model. A social practice model counteracts this by arguing that literacy, which is fundamentally about communication, is part of society and as such is a site of power relations. This implies that if there are problems, it is because access to and the practice of LLN is uneven. People are excluded from using LLN for their own ends. The deficit lies not with the individual, but with deficient and divisive systems of education, and values that perpetuate inequality. I argue that enabling skills to develop is critical to reducing inequality. It is how they are learned and practised which matters. Learning literacy is about conceptual, social, cultural, emancipatory, technical and mechanical processes, and therefore about skills as well as social and cultural inclusivity. The sustained success of a literacy policy depends on enabling inclusive approaches to practice.

The context of this chapter is UK educational policy. Policymaking in literacy, numeracy and language, for children and adults has been a high priority across both the developed and the 'developing' world since the 1990s. Following the OECD's publication of the results of the International Adult Literacy Survey in 1998, and the subsequent international PISA studies of 15 year olds, a number of countries have created high-profile, funded policies. In the case of the countries of Britain, each of the four administrations has responded with a strategy for post-16 literacy, numeracy and ESOL. Through the Skills for Life strategy in England, over £1.5 billion had been spent by 2004 in an effort to meet a numerical target of 2.25 million people raising their literacy by one officially defined level by 2010. This level of commitment to adult literacy, numeracy and ESOL policy is unprecedented.

## Informing policy – challenges and potential rewards

Informing policy is a complex and difficult business. As Ben Levin has argued (Levin 2005), it is difficult to understand policy dynamics from outside; many people have negative views of policy: that it is too short term, expecting results within electoral cycles; cynical, and interfering. A more positive view is that policy prioritization is an open way of allocating resources and enables change. Policy priorities change quickly, based more on competing forces, beliefs, and the personal experience and values of policymakers, than on evidence. However, we are in an era where there is a public policy commitment to evidence-informed decision taking. Governments want to know 'what works', they want results and they want good feedback from the electorate about the impact of policy initiatives. These are challenges: new evidence usually takes longer to gather and analyse than the electoral cycle. But there are opportunities, because LLN has become a major policy priority for the first time since the 19th century. It seems set to stay as a policy commitment. It needs to, if hard cultural and social divisions are to reduce.

Why does informing policy of the value of socio-cultural approaches to literacy, language and numeracy matter? I suggest four reasons below. There are more. First, literacy, informally developed and used as a social practice, is part of social being in private and public spheres: at home, work and in the community. However, learning that is recognized and legitimized is undertaken overwhelmingly within the formally structured, publicly funded education system, which is shaped by policy in form and content. If LLN learning is to be useful to people and communities in daily life, how and what people learn must support and develop their practice. If learning is not 'fit for purpose' it will neither help people to gain the skills and knowledge they need, nor will it be value for money for government. Second, LLN usages are continually changing, as are the technologies and media which influence and express them. Governments need to respond to and help shape curricula, teaching and learning in ways which enable people to adapt to global changes, and learn new forms of literacy as they emerge. Governments cannot succeed by deciding alone what skills, knowledge and mindsets will support people's lives. Neither can they make learning happen: it is learners, helped by teachers and trusted others, who earn and practise LLN. They do it best if they can follow their own motivation, pursue their own purposes, supported by policy.

The third reason for the importance of socio-cultural approaches is that government strategies such as Skills for Life need them, more than they know. Strategies are often driven by economic concerns: for example, the creation of a higher skilled workforce to enable the UK to compete in a dynamic global market. The link between literacy, higher level skills, productivity, and economic health is a strong belief area in policy. Even though the link is still contested in historical and contemporary research evidence (Sanderson 1991; Wolf 2002), at policy level it is believed. Evidence is sought that strengthens the belief, rather than to consider the basis for policy approaches. It follows that the focus of learning is the acquisition of literacy, language and numeracy either as free-standing basic skills with a strong work orientation, or 'embedded' in vocational courses to support the achievement of vocational qualifications. In England learners are initially diagnosed to establish their level, with the aim of raising that level, measured by a nationally recognized qualification, assessed by an unseen test.

Consistent with its economic focus, the Skills for Life strategy, for example, aims to raise the skills of individual learners, especially young people, and employees. The strategy is explicitly geared to supporting young people and includes schools-based qualifications. Indeed, LLN qualifications for 14–19 year olds and adults are likely soon to be merged (DfES 2005) and firmly based on 'functional skills' newly designed for 14–19 year olds. The needs of older adults and anyone over 65 are invisible, despite the changing demographics of the workplace and the mathematics of pensions. Policy remains largely impervious to the importance, recognized by employers, of affective learning gains such as self-confidence, engaging with others and other so-called 'soft' skills. Policymakers have not fully recognized the potential of socio-cultural models to create wider benefits such as individual, community and social well-being, or expressed through policy that these benefits positively support employment and enterprise. This narrowness is not only attributable to the ways of policy, however. Apart from new NRDC research at Lancaster University (Barton et al. 2006; Ivanic and Tseng 2005) the practical, inclusive value of these models to the success of the policy itself has not been stressed strongly enough by practitioners or researchers to the policy community. If the two discourses and models could reach out to meet each other, a more integrated conceptual framework might be developed which recognizes the skills in social practice and the social practice in skills. This would have the potential to be much more powerful than the current, over-polarized standoff. Purposeful dialogue is urgent. Skills divorced from context, mechanically learned and crudely measured, will not be adequate to the changing demands of work or leisure. This will emerge sooner rather than later: the success of policies such as Skills for Life, will be at stake. Equally, social practice models need to be translated into clear practical applications for teacher education and classroom practice, so that they can flourish in learning settings. Neither approach has wanted enough to appreciate and learn from the other, to the detriment of learners.

Fourth, despite the dominance of economic concerns, current literacy, language and numeracy policies are also characterized by a belief that they are helping to reduce inequality and cycles of deprivation. Social inclusion is a lesser, but real focus, expressed for example in programmes to support family LLN, and offenders' rehabilitation, trade union-led initiatives, special community-focused projects. The Adult Community Learning Fund and the Trade Union Learning Fund, both part of Skills for Life in England, expose the contradictions in a policy that appears genuinely to wish to address inequality, and yet cannot escape from the tight coils of economic arguments. The result is an uneasy settlement between the economic and the social, in which a utilitarian, skills-led approach dominates. Socio-cultural approaches could make for a better balance, and large-scale qualitative evidence supports a strong policy emphasis on social, cultural and economic approaches (Barton et al. 2003; Barton et al. 2006) which would better match views and practices on the ground. A more mutually motivating partnership between policy and practice could result.

## Motivation and engagement

From the writings of adult learners in thousands of student magazines, of which *Write First Time* (1976–1986) was the most prominent UK example; and also from historical research (Howard 1991; Rose 2002; Vincent 1989), it is clear that learners have always been motivated or demotivated by other people in meaningful social processes – in the family, at work, in communities. It is still true (Brandt 2001; Padmore 1994). They are also motivated by the wish to belong to a culture from which they may feel excluded and to express their own culture as people who write, including letters to family members or prospective employers; bills, transactions, poems, diaries, lists for self and others on paper or website, reports of meetings (Barton and Hamilton 1998; Morley and Worpole 1982). Separating skill from social or cultural purposes is difficult and fruitless. But the complexity of needs should, on the basis of much evidence, inform learning. What can we say to policymakers about how LLN can respond to the needs, life circumstances, culture and aspirations of young people and adults?

## Learning

Social practice happens in different contexts. For people who are still learning literacy, or need to develop their LLN practices, as adults, the social and cultural practices of the classroom are vital. The three-year ethnographic study, Adult Learners' Lives, conducted by NRDC at Lancaster University shows clearly that, if learning is to be effective, it must be relevant to people's lives (Barton et al. 2003). LLN practices are situated in changing lives that create changing LLN needs. Learning is the social and dynamic process which links current and future contexts and hopes. Successful learning is dependent on strong (social) relationships between learners and between learners and teachers. The social practices model argues that all literacy and numeracy is social, expressed by 'events' and the importance of explicitly addressing social practices in the literacy classroom is emerging as critical (Ivanic and Tseng 2005). Another study reports that learners do not reject a skills-based national test, but need it to be sensitively embedded formatively in teaching and learning practice. It needs to be talked about and explained as part of the learning process, leading to other learning. Learners value the skills of patience, caring and rigour as much as the subject knowledge of teachers. These approaches, research suggests, will help learners to succeed.

Using such evidence, policy could open up the discourses in which its own 'learning infrastructure', advice and directives are couched, recognize that social practice in the classroom works, encourage group as much as individual learning, and help those who shape and deliver teacher education and professional development to use socio-cultural practice as part of a holistic system of standards and curricula. Social practice can be presented, in part, as essential to skills learning (Barton et al. forthcoming). With no resource implications, policy can be experienced more widely as a social good. A model which ignores the cultural and social nature of literacy in workplace or classroom, contrariwise, may undermine its own potential and fail to engage learners. It is becoming clear that literacy learning that draws on a social practice approach 'works', in policy terms and in addressing socio-cultural inequalities.

## Practising literacy, language and numeracy: implications for policy

In the workplace, research indicates that mathematics, writing, talking and listening are all critically important skills (Hoyles et al. 2002). Employers often comment that the 'generative skills' needed to participate at work are similar to those needed at home and in the community. Employers, the most important beneficiaries of skills for life in the policy discourse, repeatedly demand social, cultural and attitudinal attributes and skills as well as technical ones. People who relate to others, who solve problems, are creative, take initiatives, listen as well as speak, use communication technologies effectively, and so on. It appears, too, from research that the workplace can be as supportive and enabling for people previously averse to participating. Men, for example, seem to flourish in workplace learning. All this evidence suggests widening approaches to LLN are relevant to the modern workplace (Ananiadou et al. 2004). What is the advice to policy from this evidence? Curricula and assessment regimes which put active and interactive uses of literacy, language and numeracy at their heart will help people to realize their potential. This would signal an end to simplistic, multiple-choice tests, and support the development, of wider knowledge, skills, attributes and attitudes through formative assessment (Lavender, Derrick and Brooks 2004). Another message is that 'talk is work' in classrooms. In ESOL, it helps learners practise language with each other, and integrate their learning with their lives (Roberts et al. 2004); in LLN teaching and learning, talk enables interactive, reflective learning in groups, which more closely reflects real-life work settings. As it stands, the Skills for Life policy encourages teachers to focus on individuals: individual learning plans, individual work schedules and worksheet-based materials. Social interaction, including talk and noise have, it seems, diminished even though they are associated with learners' persistence and progress. NRDC's studies of 'effective practice' in LLN will shed more light on this when they report in 2006.

Recognizing learning and practice as social helps to link formal with informal learning, which exemplifies learning as social practice. Research has found that informality engages disaffected young people, including offenders. Alongside practical and vocational workshops, these groups of learners welcome interaction, personal support, respect and understanding, rather than discrete formal LLN learning reminiscent of school (Hurry and Brazier 2004; McNeil and Smith 2005). The findings raise questions for policy: is Skills for Life, in its efforts to raise the attainment of 14–19 year olds, consciously or unconsciously informed by a schools approach, in which imparting knowledge and skills, rather than interactive social practice approaches are still the fundamental model? Is a key to making the social practice case that the approach is relevant to all ages, not least disaffected young people? This research suggests so.

## LLN for social inclusion

Social inclusion remains an important policy issue, even if it is less dominant than economic imperatives. Social and cultural policy priorities nearly always include those at risk of exclusion, for ideological or resource reasons. A critical issue is whether, as in the case of Skills for Life, bringing people quickly across a threshold which is designed and delivered 'top down' is the main aim. If it is, then working with those whose problems make them most at risk in social, cultural and economic policy areas may be neglected. The danger of perpetuating social and cultural exclusion in the long term may be high, but policy works to political cycles, seeking short-term evidence of gain. A good example of possible influence is John Bynner's recent work on the 1970 cohort study of 10,000 people and their children (Bynner forthcoming). This study of literacy and numeracy shows that people whose skills, both assessed and self-reported, are at 'entry level 2' and below in the official system of levels, are clearly and significantly more affected than people just one level (entry level 3) higher. People's literacy at low levels can be correlated with other impacts on their lives such as mental health, poor job prospect and poverty. Most interestingly for policy, their children's lives, especially their literacy learning, can be adversely affected. Yet the research suggests that if they acknowledge their learning needs, the improvements to their literacy and lives can be relatively greater than people at higher levels.

Here is a challenge for policy. Research shows that many adult LLN learners take a long time to make progress, let alone attain a national qualification. Intergenerational cycles of deprivation are difficult to break. The problem is by definition long term. Yet, policymakers are interested in this research. One reason is that the policy, in the public mind, always was about such groups of people. Skills for Life policy discourses have always expressed commitment to reducing inequality, and improving life chances. But since the target has not included them, the research illuminates a policy danger: by 2010, there may still be many adults with low skills and future international surveys could show Skills for Life has not made a big enough difference. Another reason is timeliness: the finding is relevant to essential elements of Skills for Life, halfway through its lifespan. First, the 2010 target may be difficult to reach. There are potentially a lot of people at entry 2 and below, not currently engaging with the system, or even recognizing they have any problem. Perhaps the target could be reviewed and people at the lowest levels included as a priority group – a review is due shortly. Second, family LLN is a key element of Skills for Life. The ultimate focus has been on helping adults to help their children at school or early years programmes. Yet clearly, adults own skills, more widely, need to be addressed to make most meaning out of family LLN. Third, this is a cross-government policy: related policies for children and young people may depend on adults' learning to succeed. Finally, economic arguments are always prominent. Millions of adults with such low skills are more likely to be dependent on the state, suffer health and relationship problems, and can help their children learn only with difficulty, even if 63 percent try to (DfES 2003). Their situation is a policy challenge. At periods of high employment, this inequality of access to LLN is easier to ignore. When economic prospects are gloomier, developing the capabilities of those most likely to depend on state support becomes a more pressing issue. Add to this demographic trends which will see adults working through their 60s and even 70s, and the lifelong literacy learning should be centre stage, although it is not yet so.

## Role of research and the voices of learners

I have drawn largely on research as a way of informing policy. There have been nearly 10 years of government commitment to increased funding of research and a more evidence-based approach to policy development. While this is welcome, quantitative research and evaluations of large-scale national initiatives dominate other approaches. Yet it is clear that numbers alone are not enough to convince policymakers. Policymakers need the hard data for the Treasury, but human experience, even at anecdotal level, ranks high in policymaking and is a way of relating to voters. Voters count.

Socio-cultural approaches bring out the authenticity of lived experience as well as the impact of inequality, offering meaning and depth to quantitative work. Ethnography, life history and case study approaches to research help policy because they explain and bring alive research when it is being promoted at policy level. They lend rigour to the familiarity of story and anecdote. As Levin (2005) has argued, humans need stories to grasp meaning and see what change it implies. Numbers alone cannot be 'read', understood, or plugged into belief systems that drive policy, without accompanying stories. The most effective stories are from learners, who can show what LLN means in their lives and work and what changes can be wrought by learning.

Research is critical to informing policy in one other way. It is, itself, part of the social and cultural practices it addresses. The best researchers talk, listen, read, write, calculate, estimate and form judgements by working with others, including policymakers and those stakeholders who can influence policy and create change. Teacher–researchers, managers, teacher trainers, inspectors, employers, unions, other researchers and developers and learners are all critical to active research relationships. As Levin argues, relationships of trust are essential for policy change. Research produced in partnership is, at best, a unique combination of 'stories' with 'numbers', inflected and shaped by knowledge collected and analysed from a wide variety of perspectives. Quantitative and qualitative research are more powerful ways of influencing policy if they work together to create 'stories with numbers' rather than work separately (Levin 2005). This approach offers the policy community ways to engage positively with their concerns. As a social and cultural practice, it is a three-way dialogue between those with little power, those intermediaries with the ability to influence, and the powerful themselves. This is one way to begin to break down barriers and address real concerns about who gets to learn and use LLN, speak and be heard in our society.

# References

Ananiadou, K., Emslie-Henry, R., Evans, K. and Wolf, A. (2004) 'Identifying effective workplace basic skills strategies enhancing employee productivity and development', downloadable from www.nrdc.org.uk.

Barton, D. and Hamilton, M. (1998) *Local Literacies: Reading and Writing in One Community*. London: Routledge.

Barton, D., Ivanic, R., Appleby, V., Hodge, R. and Tusting, K. (2003) 'Adult learners' lives: setting the scene', downloadable from www.nrdc.org.uk.

Barton, D., Ivanic, R., Appleby, V., Hodge, R. and Tusting, K. (2006) 'Relating lives and learning: adults' engagement in community settings', will be downloadable from www.nrdc.org.uk.

Bourdieu, P. (1993) *The Field of Cultural Production*. Columbia, SC: Columbia University Press.

Brandt, D. (2001) *Literacy in American Lives*. Cambridge: Cambridge University Press.

Bynner, J. (forthcoming) *New Light on Literacy and Numeracy*, will be downloadable from www.nrdc.org.uk.

DfES (2003) *The Skills for Life Survey: A National Needs and Impact Survey of Literacy, Numeracy and ICT Skills*. London: DfES.

DfES (2005) *Education and Skills 14–19 White Paper*. London: DfES.

Howard, U. (1991) 'Self, education, and writing in nineteenth-century English communities' in Barton, D. and Ivanic, R. (eds) *Writing in the Community*. London, Sage.

Hoyles, C., Wolf, A., Molyneux-Hodgson, S. and Kent, P. (2002) *Mathematical Skills in the Workplace*. London: The Science, Technology and Mathematics Council. [Also downloadable from www.ioe. ac.uk/tlrp/technomaths/skills2002.]

Hurry, J. and Brazier, L. (2004) 'Improving the literacy and numeracy of disaffected young people in custody and in the community', downloadable from www.nrdc.org.uk.

Ivanic, R. and Tseng, M. (2005) 'Understanding the relationships between learning and teaching: an analysis of the contribution of applied linguistics', downloadable from www.nrdc.org.uk.

Lavender, P., Derrick, J. and Brooks, B. (2004) *Testing, Testing 1,2,3*. Leicester: NIACE.

Levin, B. (2005) 'Connecting research and practice in reflect 2 NRDC'; 'How governments make policy choices', conference presentation, NRDC, downloadable from www.nrdc.org.uk.

McNeil, B. and Smith, L. (2005) 'Success factors in informal learning: young people's experience of literacy, language and numeracy, will be downloadable from www.nrdc.org.uk.

Morley, D. and Worpole, K. (eds) (1982) *The Republic of Letters: Working Class Writing and Local Publishing*. London: Comedia Publishing Group.

Padmore S. (1994) 'Guiding lights' in Hamilton, M., Barton, D. and Ivanic, R. (eds) *Worlds of Literacy*. Clevedon: Multilingual Matters.

Roberts, C., Baynham, W., Shrubshall, P., Barton, D., Chopra, P., Cooke, M., Hodge, R., Pitt, K., Schellekens, P., Wallace, C. and Whitfield, S. (2004) 'English for speakers of other languages: case studies of provision, learners' needs and resources, downloadable from *www.nrdc.org.uk.*

Rose, J. (2002) *The Intellectual Life of the British Working Classes*. New Haven, NJ: Yale University Press.

Sanderson, M. (1991) *Economic Change and Society in England 1780–1870*. Basingstoke: Macmillan Education.

Vincent, D. (1989) *Literacy and Popular Culture: England 1750–1914*. Cambridge: Cambridge University Press.

Williams, R. (1961) *The Long Revolution*. London: Columbia University Press.

Williams, R. (1981) *Culture*. London: Fontana.

Williams, R. (1984) *Writing in Society*. London: Verso.

Wolf, A. (2002) *Does Education Matter? Myths about Education and Economic Growth*. London: Penguin Books.

*Write First Time* (1976–1986) A quarterly broadsheet of literacy students' writing. The *Write First Time* archive is held at Ruskin College, Oxford.

# 4 Adult Literacies and Social Inclusion: Practice, Research and Policy in Scotland

*Lyn Tett*

## Social inclusion

The term 'social exclusion' came into common use through a number of EU, UK and Scottish policy documents (CEC 2000; DfEE 1998; Scottish Executive 1998) in the late 20th century:

> [However], the excluded do not constitute a defined group in the population: there is no single clear-cut definition of 'social exclusion'. Categories such as the 'unskilled' 'ethnic minorities' 'the unemployed' cover a range of circumstances. ... So 'exclusion' does not bring a precise target into view but a range of associated issues. (OECD 1999: 15–16)

Generally, the term has been associated with the long-established and deep-rooted problems of poverty and unemployment that have been exacerbated by growing social and economic inequalities. In response to these problems, the stated aim of the social inclusion policies of governments is to ensure that all citizens, whatever their social or economic background, have opportunities to participate fully in society and enjoy a high quality of life. It is suggested that education and lifelong learning have a central role to play in this process because lifelong learning programmes have the potential to 'change people's lives, even transform them' (Fryer 1997: 24), particularly through enabling people to participate in the labour market.

The part that the state is to play in combating social exclusion and promoting lifelong learning is, however, more ambiguous. The impact of globalizing tendencies in the economy and culture and the associated trends towards individualism and declining support for welfarism have led governments to seek the promotion of more active and engaged citizens. The goal of policy is now to change behaviour in civil society (individuals and organizations) rather than simply provide a service. As Rhodes (1996: 655) has argued the management of contemporary states involves ' "less government" (or less rowing) but "more governance" (or more steering)'. Similarly, John Field has argued that the use of the term 'social exclusion' throughout western Europe reflects a policy change. He suggests that 'rather than struggling against the social causes of inequality, the new language of exclusion implies that government's task is to promote "inclusion" into the existing social order' (Field 2000: 108).

## Literacies and social inclusion

Literacy and numeracy skills have assumed enormous significance in contemporary western society as both a cause of social exclusion and a solution to social inclusion. Being literate and numerate is generally equated with success in life, with notions of a person being 'educated', obtaining a job and having access to the 'goods' and trappings of well-being that are valued highly in society. Policies across the world commonly assume that lack of literacy and numeracy restricts the ability of workers to adapt to new technology and new workplace practices, and leads to safety concerns, costly mistakes and a host of other negative features. For example, the English Moser Report (Moser 1999) makes explicit the economic implications of low literacy and numeracy skills, and in the United States and Australia improving the literacy skills of workers has long been regarded as integral to economic development (for example, Chisman and Campbell 1990; DEET 1992). The international OECD reports all strongly recommend a focus on improving literacy skills as the 'key' to unlocking the benefits of globalization (for example, OECD 1995: 23).

One impact of the effects of globalization has been to see the nation-state as having diminishing powers and so there is little opportunity to intervene except through promoting education and training as a source of sustainable competition (Tett 2002). In this new context issues of socioeconomic inequality and the concern for wealth redistribution as part of a programme of social justice, have been seen as less important and ideas about how inequalities are viewed have changed. This means that appeals for greater spending to alleviate poverty and promote social justice are often couched in terms of assuaging middle-class fears of the poor and as an investment, rather than a gift (Phillips 1999). A corollary of these approaches is that rather than government doing things directly, it is required to persuade citizens to change their ways. Thus in the field of literacy and numeracy, government has encouraged a widespread search for 'active measures' that place responsibilities on citizens to plan and develop themselves, for example, by taking part in training and education (Coffield 1999).

So improving literacy and numeracy skills has become an important social inclusion policy that stresses individual responsibility for taking action to change existing deficits. Literacy and numeracy are treated, however, as if they were a set of unproblematic, information-processing cognitive skills that are independent of the context in which they are used. This approach has framed the terms of the debate, defined the scope and content of which groups are seen to be deficient in literacy and numeracy and why, and denied the central role of culture and relationships of power in determining literacy and numeracy needs and aspirations. Literacy and numeracy skills are seen as neutral and objective within a discourse that takes no account of the ways in which they are used in specific communities. In this discourse, 'literacy skills are elevated; they are viewed as a set of technical skills which, once acquired, usually lead to positive employment outcomes' (Black 2002: 2).

In contrast, ethnographic studies of literacy and numeracy practices reveal the role of social networks where people act as 'mediators' or 'brokers' in assisting others (Barton and Hamilton 1998; Baynham 1993). This analysis leads Stephen Black to suggest that 'where there is a need to improve literacy and numeracy practices in workplaces, this can often be accomplished effectively through informal networks of assistance from fellow workers' (Black 2002). That is, workers in 'communities of practice', learning through a process of 'apprenticeship' from more experienced and skilled workers (see Billett 1999; Lankshear 1998; Lave and Wenger 1991; Wenger 1998).

From this ethnographic analysis it appears that although there is a clear correlation between good literacy and numeracy skills and obtaining and retaining employment, as a means of social inclusion, it is based on a deficit model of the learner within a discourse of individual responsibility. An alternative approach is to focus on developing social processes and practices that can counteract the low self-esteem of learners and encourage a collective approach to sharing skills and knowledge. This approach would also tackle the low expectations of employers who sometimes seem to use literacy and numeracy as a proxy for screening people out even though the skills tested may not be the ones required for the job (see Quigley 1997). For example, years of schooling and school leaving qualifications are often given much higher status that practical skills gained from experience even though these very skills are the ones that people need to do the particular job.

Is it possible to move to move from the dominant, deficit, approach to literacy and numeracy as a way of more effectively promoting social inclusion and justice for all? In the following section, I explore the ways in which practitioners and researchers worked together to develop a social practices approach and sought to embed it in the ALN curriculum through influencing policymakers in Scotland.

## Practice, research and policy in Scotland

A number of researchers (for example, Mentor, Mahoney and Hextall 2004; Paterson 2000) have argued that the longstanding enthusiasm for national social development in Scotland has led to a greater confidence in the professionalism of teachers and other educators than is evident, for example, in England. This has resulted in a more consensual form of consultation about educational developments and the involvement of 'insider' practitioner–experts in assisting the Scottish Executive in developing policy documents and practice guides for use in educational settings. In the case of the adult literacy and numeracy curriculum, a literacies practitioner was seconded to the Executive from one of the local authorities in 1999 in order to develop materials and a system that would be appropriate to the Scottish context, followed by the appointment of a task group 'Literacy 2000' that also comprised practitioners and policymakers. These actions resulted in a different approach to that used by England and Wales being advocated and then developed in key policy documents that set out the quality framework to be used in implementing and evaluating literacy and numeracy provision (for example, City of Edinburgh Council/ Scottish Executive 2000). The key difference was the development of a social practices approach to ALN that was regarded as more appropriate to the community-based context of provision in Scotland. This approach views learning as situated in concrete social practices and as a result it can only be understood by making reference to those knowledge structures, discourses and practices that reflect particular time and space bound concerns of individual communities (see Scott 2001).

The Scottish policy agenda for developing literacies has also been informed by issues of social justice, equality, and democracy in everyday life. For example, a key literacies policy document recognized some of the problems associated with a deficit approach to learning and instead advocated a 'lifelong learning approach'. The policy suggests that this approach:

> Rather than focusing on a minimum standard, is concerned more with establishing what the learner's goals are. ... The aim is to access learners' ability to apply their learning to real contexts and to measure the economic, personal and social gains that they make, including their willingness to learn in the future. (Scottish Executive 2001: 14)

Such policies provided opportunities for literacy programmes to be grounded in the life situations of adults and communities in response to issues that are derived from their own knowledge. It thus provides an alternative model of lifelong learning that contributes towards a more socially just society.

Since the original appointment of a practitioner and the publication of the subsequent policy documents, researchers and practitioners have continued to work together to inform and challenge the Scottish Executive in a number of ways. First, through advocating the importance of providing opportunities for educators to ground literacy programmes in the life situations of adults and communities in response to issues that are derived from their own interests and knowledge. This approach reflects the values of literacies work in communities of access and equality that informs the Scottish approach and is now embedded in the quality framework. For example, the criteria for entry pathways are that 'access is prompt and easy and the programme is open to potential learners with needs and aspirations in any area of adult life' (City of Edinburgh Council/Scottish Executive 2000: 11).

A second area has been through the development of the ALN curriculum that places an emphasis on how people *use* literacy rather than why other people think they *need* these skills. For example, the key Scottish Executive policy paper, *Adult Literacy and Numeracy in Scotland*, defined literacies as: 'The ability to read, write and use numbers, to handle information, express ideas and opinions, make decisions and solve problems, as family members, workers, citizens and lifelong learners' (Scottish Executive 2001).

The definition shows that:

- To be literate and numerate is not only to have the mechanical skills of encoding and decoding symbols but also the knowledge, skills and understanding that enable us to do what we want to do in our private, family, community, and working lives.
- The key life areas and social contexts in which literacy and numeracy are used are important in deciding on what is to be learned.
- Literacy and numeracy skills are almost always employed for a purpose – such as making decisions or solving problems – and in a particular social context. The use of literacy and numeracy in everyday life is closely linked with social practices that have their own social purpose and meaning. The incidental learning that happens in such contexts is as important as planned and deliberate learning within the learning programme. It is important that learners not only develop skills in a particular

context but also become proficient in other contexts in order to broaden and transfer their learning.

The underpinning approach is made even more explicit in the document that sets out the ALN Curriculum Framework (Scottish Executive 2005) that was developed by a group of practitioners and researchers. It states:

> We are using a *social practices* account of adult literacy and numeracy. Rather than seeing literacy and numeracy as the decontextualized, mechanical, manipulation of letters, words and figures this view shows that literacy and numeracy are located within social, emotional and linguistic contexts. Many literacy and numeracy events in life are regular, repeated activities, such as paying bills, sending greetings cards, reading bed-time stories and some events are linked into routine sequences that are part of the formal procedures and expectations of social institutions such as work-places, schools and welfare agencies. The more informal expectations and pressures of the home or peer group structure other events where there are expectations about the right way to do things. Literacy and numeracy practices integrate the routines, skills, and understandings, that are organized within specific contexts and also the feelings and values that people have about these activities. If you are worried that you can't do something then you are going to find it more difficult in a public or workplace context than if you were at home in a relaxed situation (Scottish Executive 2005: 3)

Researchers and practitioners have shown policymakers that using a theory of learning that emphasizes social participation as one of the key processes of learning and knowing can encourage deep learning (Wenger 1998). Rather than seeing learning as a process whereby an individual learner internalizes knowledge that is largely cerebral, this perspective presupposes action and participation as a member of a socio-cultural community of practice. People participate in these 'communities of practice' all the time, at work, in communities, in the family and so on. Learning programmes that are grounded in these life situations can encourage participation by responding to issues that are derived from people's own interests, knowledge, expertise and experience of the world. This is much more likely to encourage learning that has value to those that use it. It is important to remember, however, that these practices are set within particular power regimes and always involve a struggle over whose knowledge are privileged and whose are denigrated. Staying within the known and safe regimes of action is always the easiest option and challenging these institutionalized ways of doing things is difficult.

This social practices approach to ALN has also led to funding regimes that focus to some extent on opportunities rather than outcomes. For example, the expansion of the supply side of learning opportunities to a wider range of groups, such as young people, than have previously participated in literacies provision is one aspect of the way in which the literacies initiative addresses equality of opportunity. By the same token, the evaluation of the impact of the strategy on learners has been based on numbers participating and learning gains in terms of 'distance travelled', an equality of outcomes approach. Again this shows the influence of researchers and practitioners in establishing appropriate outcomes as most of the other educational interventions such as new community schools or the 'New Deal' have used hard indicators such as increases in qualifications or employment outcomes. Again, however, these are issues that are struggled over as qualifications and employment are much easier to measure than distance travelled. A balance has to be set between what is feasible within the limited time that practitioners have to provide evidence of achievement and the demands of external bodies for evidence of learning gains.

In using soft indicators, including learners' assessments of what they had gained from their programmes such as increases in self-esteem and the ability to use their skills, knowledge and understanding in a range of contexts, the new provision has benefited from a more appropriate evaluation. This strategy was established in the spirit of the social justice approach that prioritized learners' views as the most important in assessing the success of programmes. To this end the Scottish Executive (2003) commissioned a two-year study of literacy and numeracy learners' views about their experiences of participating in programmes as its key way of evaluating its additional expenditure. This study has used the quality framework (City of Edinburgh Council/Scottish Executive 2000) as the instrument against which to assess learners' views of their provision. So the cycle of practitioners influencing policy, which is interpreted by researchers, using the views of learners who in turn influence policy, is set in motion. Caution is needed here too in making too grand claims as policymakers are often rather selective in what they are willing to accept as evidence from research despite an avowed commitment to evidence-based policy development.

## Social inclusion and a 'social practices' approach

I have outlined how the social practices view of literacy and numeracy became embedded in the Scottish ALN curriculum. I believe that if this approach is set within a social justice context then it can make an important contribution to social inclusion. Some ways in which this might be done, and to some extent have already been achieved in Scotland, are:

- literacy and numeracy being organized within specific social, emotional and linguistic contexts that integrate feelings, values, routines, skills, understandings, and activities
- purposeful learning that builds on learners' prior knowledge and experience to shape and construct new knowledge but also challenges them to take risks
- developing a curriculum that helps students to recognize that they have the capacity to learn and to generate new knowledge that will be really useful to them
- working on both increasing skills and developing people's critical awareness of why they might not have these skills in the first place
- using learning to increase individual and collective self-confidence
- developing the awareness of employers, policymakers and other decision makers about the value of using a 'social practices', rather than a deficit, approach to literacy and numeracy.

Learning programmes that are grounded in people's life situations are much more likely to encourage learning that has value to those that use it. This is equally true for practitioners participating in professional development courses. When people create their own knowledge and have their voices heard, narrow definitions of what is thought to be 'educated knowledge' and who it is that makes it, are thrown into question. Learners and practitioners alike need to have their knowledge valued and built on so embedding a social practice approach into professional development is an important goal. One way of challenging existing knowledge is through enquiry-based projects that value the experience that practitioners bring to research and practice. In these ways, the experiences and stories of learners and practitioners that have been excluded, because they do not fit into the dominant way of thinking, can be foregrounded. Only feeling able to say what others have said, rather than what they want to say, can silence people. Therefore a commitment to emphasizing the wealth of people's knowledge rather than pointing out their deficits is necessary. This involves valuing difference and building a curriculum that starts from people's everyday uses, meanings and purposes for reading and writing and developing authentic texts that reflect the reality of their everyday lives (see Barr 1999). This can provide a hope for a better life than the one currently experienced so the risks of learning can be outweighed by the desire for change. In this sense, education's proper role is to stir the imagination and challenge comfortable habits in ways that open up more democratic visions for the future. It is important to begin questioning limitations in order to explore what is possible for the future. It can also mean experiencing unacceptably high levels of discontinuity and risk too. It is important then that learning both draws on people's existing knowledge and experiences but also challenges them to go beyond the familiar.

## Conclusion

This chapter has attempted to show how practice and research has informed policy in order to promote social inclusion and justice for all. However, changing the arrangements of learning as well as people's perceptions of it are an enormous and costly undertaking yet much of the work that goes on in literacies is under-funded with the lowest ratio of paid teaching staff to learners found in community-based provision (see Tett 2004). This under-funding needs to be challenged and this calls for a new alliance of practitioners and researchers to work together for change.

The personal and social damage inflicted by inequality, social exclusion and restricted opportunity is immense. An important component of social inclusion is learning that should represent a resource for people to help them identify inequalities, probe their origins and begin to challenge them, using skills, information and knowledge in order to achieve and stimulate change. Through this type of learning, the production of knowledge is put back into the hands of people, competing values can be thought about and their relevance for people's lives can be assessed (see Fryer 1997). Clearly, while learning alone certainly cannot abolish the deep-rooted causes of social exclusion it can make a useful contribution to combating it, not least by tackling the ways in which social exclusion is reinforced through the very processes and outcomes of some types of literacy and numeracy education.

# References

Barr, J. (1999) 'Women, adult education and really useful knowledge' in Crowther, J., Martin, I. and Shaw, M. (eds) *Popular Education and Social Movements in Scotland Today*. Leicester: NIACE.

Barton, D. and Hamilton, M. (1998) *Local Literacies: Reading and Writing in One Community*. London: Sage.

Baynham, M. (1993) Code switching and mode switching: community interpreters and mediators of literacy' in Street, B. (ed.) *Cross-cultural Approaches to Literacy*. Cambridge: Cambridge University Press.

Billett, S. (1999) 'Guided learning at work' in Boud, D. and Garrick, J. (eds) *Understanding Learning at Work*. London: Routledge.

Black, S. (2002) 'Whose economic well-being? A challenge to dominant discourses on the relationship between literacy and numeracy skills and (un)employment', downloadable from www.staff.vu.edu/alnarc/onlineforum/AL-pap-black.htm (accessed 30 June 2005).

Chisman, F. and Campbell, W. (1990) 'Narrowing the jobs-skills gap: a focus on workplace literacy' in Chisman, F. (ed.) *Leadership for Literacy: The Agenda for the 1990s*. San Francisco: Jossey Bass.

City of Edinburgh Council/Scottish Executive (CEC/SE) (2000) *Literacies in the Community*. Edinburgh: City of Edinburgh Council.

Coffield, F. (1999) 'Breaking the consensus: lifelong learning as social control'. *British Educational Research Journal*, 25(4): 479–99.

Commission of the European Communities (CEC) (2000) *A Memorandum on Lifelong Learning*. Brussels: Directorate General for Education, Training and Youth.

Department for Education and Employment (DfEE) (1998) *The Learning Age – A Renaissance for a New Britain*. London: The Stationery Office.

Department of Employment, Education and Training (DEET) (1992) *Getting the Word Out: The Australian Language and Literacy Policy*. Canberra: AGPS.

Field, J. (2000) *Lifelong Learning and the New Educational Order*. Stoke-on-Trent: Trentham Books.

Fryer, R.H. (1997) *Learning for the Twenty First Century*. London: DfEE.

Lankshear, C. (1998) 'Frameworks and work frames: literacy policies and new orders'. *Unicorn*, 24(2): 43–58.

Lave, J. and Wenger, E. (1991) *Situated Learning: Legitimate Peripheral Participation*. Cambridge: Cambridge University Press.

Mentor, I., Mahoney, P. and Hextall, I. (2004) 'Ne'er the twain shall meet? Modernizing the teaching profession in Scotland and England'. *Journal of Education Policy*, 19: 2.

Moser, C. (1999) *A Fresh Start: Improving Literacy and Numeracy*. London: DFEE.

OECD (1995) *Literacy, Economy and Society.* Paris: OECD.

OECD (1999) *Overcoming Social Exclusion through Adult Learning.* Paris: OECD.

Paterson, L. (2000) 'Traditions of Scottish education' in Holmes, H. (ed.) *Education (Volume 11 of Scottish Life and Society).* East Lothian: Tuckwell Press.

Phillips, A. (1999) *Which Equalities Matter?* Cambridge: Polity Press.

Quigley, A. (1997) *Rethinking Literacy Education.* San Francisco: Jossey Bass.

Rhodes, R.A.W. (1996) 'The new governance: governing without government'. *Political Studies,* 44(4): 652–67.

Scott, D. (2001) 'Situated views of learning' in Paechter, C., Edwards, R., Harrison, R. and Twining, P. (eds) *Learning, Space and Identity.* London: Paul Chapman.

Scottish Executive (1998) *Opportunity Scotland: A Paper on Lifelong Learning.* Edinburgh: The Stationery Office.

Scottish Executive (2001) *Adult Literacy and Numeracy in Scotland.* Edinburgh: The Stationery Office.

Scottish Executive (2003) *Evaluating the Adult Literacy and Numeracy Curriculum for Scotland.* Edinburgh: The Stationery Office.

Scottish Executive (2005) *An Adult Literacy and Numeracy Curriculum Framework for Scotland.* Edinburgh: The Stationery Office.

Tett, L. (2002) *Community Education, Lifelong Learning and Social Inclusion.* Edinburgh: Dunedin Academic Press.

Tett, L. (2004) 'Literacy, learning and social inclusion' in Proceedings of the 4th ESREA Research Conference Sections 3–4, Wroclaw, Poland: ESREA.

Wenger, E. (1998) *Communities of Practice: Learning, Meaning and Identity.* Cambridge: Cambridge University Press.

# Section Two
## Literacy, Language and Multilingualism

# 5 Aligning Socio-cultural and Critical Approaches to Multilingual Literacy Research

*Elsa Auerbach*

A socio-cultural model of literacy is often seen, by definition, to challenge existing relations of power. Street argues that this model (which he calls an ideological view) 'begins from the premise that variable literacy practices are always rooted in power relations and that the apparent innocence and neutrality of the "rules" serve to disguise the ways in which such power is maintained through literacy' (Street 1996: 5). Because it recognizes the culturally variable nature of literacy practices, and questions the privileging of dominant practices, it 'draws attention to the unequal and hierarchical nature of literacy in practice' (Street 1996: 5). As such, research into the culture-specific literacy practices of non-dominant social groups is often framed as critical by virtue of its role in unmasking and challenging social hierarchies.

In this chapter, I would like to both acknowledge the seismic shift in conceptualizing literacy research that this perspective has triggered, and at the same time question whether, in practice, this research inevitably enacts a critical stance. The question driving my own work is: how can adult literacy pedagogy (with a particular focus on ESOL) contribute to building a more just world? So, for me, the horse that pulls the cart is an activist, social justice and social change agenda rather than a literacy research agenda per se. My own work is inspired by a Freirean critical theory of literacy; as such, I am interested in social practices research to the extent that it enables learners to act on their own behalf to challenge inequities and change conditions of their lives – without assuming that it always and necessarily does so. I do not take it as a given that a social practices research paradigm is, inherently, productive in moving toward change for bilingual and ESOL students or communities. Rather, I think we need to interrogate the paradigm and unpack its functions in light of broader questions of power and social change so that we can then envision how research can contribute to change. In this chapter, I will posit that social practices research *of a particular variety* can lead in this direction, that a social theory of literacy and a Freire-inspired critical theory of literacy can find points of alignment, if not congruence.

As one step in trying to sort this out, I propose to look at socio-cultural research in light of the very questions the research paradigm itself asks in investigating literacy practices. In this chapter, I begin to apply the tools of analysis used in researching *literacy* practices to interrogate *research* practices within that paradigm itself. So, while I will briefly note findings related to key concepts in the socio-cultural literacy research – domains, practices, roles, and functions – for multilingual contexts, the primary focus of my comments will be on how these categories can be applied to the literacy research paradigm itself. From there, I'll go on to suggest ways that specific kinds of social practices research can be linked to a social change agenda.

## Focuses of socio-cultural research on language, literacy and bilingualism

While language/literacy research in cognitive traditions looks at individual mental processes, the socio-cultural paradigm stresses the role of contextual, social factors in literacy acquisition and usage. Findings from this research suggest that people acquire language and literacy by being informally socialized into the practices and values of contexts in which they are immersed. As such, much of the focus of research related to multilingual literacies has shifted from school settings to domains such as homes, communities, workplaces, and religious institutions. The array of literacy practices that have been studied is far too vast to enumerate here. It includes interactions around texts in a range of domains, didactic encounters, community advocacy and democratic participation practices, ways of dealing with bureaucracies, print-managing practices of those with minimal literacy proficiency, workplace practices, gendered differences in literacy practices, etc. (cf. Goldstein 1997; Klassen 1991; Martin-Jones and Jones 2000). From this research, it is clear that values and practices regarding interactions around texts are culture specific, patterned and variable, that oral bases of literacy (for example, storytelling, religious practices) contribute to and shape literacy acquisition, and that language choice in multilingual contexts is often related to language function.

A great deal of the social practices research on multilingual literacies focuses on families and family roles in literacy events – on the distribution of practices within families: who does what with whom, why, and in which languages (cf. Anderson et al. 2005; Gregory 1998; Martin-Jones and Jones 2000; Rockhill 1993). Examinations of roles of parents and children has shown, for example, that:

- Children often act as literacy brokers or mediators in multi-lingual situations, reversing traditional parent–child power relationships and challenging taken for granted notions about the directionality of parent–child interactions.
- Siblings often play as great a role as parents in fostering each other's literacy acquisition.
- The distribution of practices in families is often gendered, shaped by values and power relationships.
- First language literacy proficiencies and second language acquisition are related in complex ways.

This research has, in turn, yielded contrastive studies that examine the relationship between dominant, school-based practices and those of non-dominant multilingual families (cf. Moll 1992). Taken together, this research suggests that the idea that there's a universal set of basic literacy skills does not hold up. Within this framework, typical school-based literacy is seen as just one of many kinds of literacy, namely, the one that comes closest to the literacy practices of socially powerful communities. This view hypothesizes that one source of educational problems for language minority learners is the fact that only one particular set of literacy practices is valued and elevated to the status of the universal standard, not because of any inherent value, but because it's the discourse of those in power (for example, Gee 1996; Heath 1983; Street 1984).

## Characteristics of the socio-cultural research paradigm

After this very truncated summary of socio-cultural research on language, literacy and bilingualism, I now turn to analysing the research paradigm itself, asking: where does the research take place? How does it take place? Who does this research? With whom? About whom? For whom? What are the functions of this research? And, finally, who benefits from it?

### Research domains

The primary domain for socio-cultural research is academic: the research often emanates from universities, is framed in academic discourses, and has academic audiences. In some cases, studies originate in governmental institutions and are designed to influence policy (for example, Stein 1997). Investigations of literacy, language and bilingualism may also be conducted as part of a pedagogical process, and incorporated into classroom practices (Roberts et al. 2001). It is rare that the domain for the research is a community-based organization; one example in the USA was the investigation of language use in community contexts conducted by participants in El Barrio Popular in NYC (Rivera 1999).

### Research practices

Extended ethnographic studies which incorporate an array of research practices are utilized in socio-cultural research on literacy. These include:

- *Observation and participant observation*: researchers position themselves either as insiders or outsiders in multilingual contexts and record observations. More often than not, the observation is done by outsiders to a multilingual community with the assistance of insiders (who often act as linguistic and cultural interpreters).
- *Interviews*: researchers interview literacy/language learners/users to find out about their practices and their understandings.
- *Inventories*: either researchers or bilingual learners/users chart data from specific domains, collecting information on artefacts, functions, participants, and so on.
- *Surveys*: researchers use questionnaires about domains, practices, roles and functions of literacy.
- *Diary studies*: researchers, teachers, and/or language/literacy learners write accounts and reflections.
- *Photography*: researchers and/or community members photograph artefacts, domains, and/or events.
- *Community maps*: researchers or community members chart key domains/sites for literacy interactions.

### Research roles

As suggested above, there can be a wide array of roles among participants in the research:

- *University-based researchers investigating practices in cultural/linguistic contexts where they are outsiders*: the research is done by 'experts'; the subjects of the research participate by providing data. Brokers or mediators (insiders who can make connections, 'translate' culture, and so on) assist the researchers.
- *University-based researchers investigating linguistic and cultural contexts in their own communities*: researchers are insiders (in

some regards) to the groups being researched. Again, the research is done by academics; often, however, these researchers draw on multiple identities in doing this research.

- *Teachers researching literacy practices of learners or learners' families*: here, teachers are trained to research the domains of students and learning from/about those they are investigating. The balance of expertise shifts, with teachers often learning from students/parents.
- *Learners researching literacy practices*: here, learners are taught to investigate the language/literacy practices within their own families, workplaces, religious institutions, communities as part of the language/literacy acquisition process.
- *Community members researching language/literacy in their own communities*: here communities may identify a concern which affects them and investigate practices related to that concern.

In some cases, the research is individual, in others collaborative. Participants from multilingual communities may be the 'subjects' of research, mediators/brokers, sources of expert knowledge, researchers, or community activists conducting research in service of some other purpose. Their involvement with the interpretation of data may take a variety of forms, from none at all, to reviewer of findings, to collaborator, to analyst. Again, the line between researcher and research subject may be blurred, with a multiplicity of identities coming into play.

### Research functions

A spectrum of functions parallels the range of practices and roles in socio cultural approaches to literacy research:

- *Shaping theory*: early extended ethnographic studies of literacy in multilingual contexts served to reshape literacy theory: they contributed to shifting the paradigm in literacy studies. Included among the theoretical claims challenged by this research were the claims that literacy itself results in enhanced cognitive functioning, that oral and written discourse are separated by a great divide, and that literacy acquisition processes are universal (Heath 1983; Scribner and Cole 1981; Street 1984).
- *Challenging beliefs*: a second, related function of this research is to denaturalize and challenge dominant beliefs: for example, numerous studies of the home literacy practices of immigrants demonstrate that, contrary to teachers' perceptions, the families value literacy and education and go to great lengths to support

their children, even when the parents themselves have minimal reading/writing proficiency. The flipside of this is that close examination of actual literacy use in multilingual contexts often denaturalizes taken for granted practices of non-immigrant, dominant groups: by unearthing and naming previously invisible literacies, the research shows that the literacy acquisition process of dominant groups, assumed to be 'normal' or natural, is but one among many ways of acquiring/using literacy.

- *Informing pedagogy*: researchers often investigate home and community contexts of bilingual children in order to learn about practices that may be incorporated into schooling. A focus of debate is whether the findings of the research should be used as a bridge to dominant literacies or as a tool for transforming school practices. In either case, the starting point for teaching is seen to be a stance of inquiry: the first task of educators is to find out about students' ways of learning and cultural contexts. Teachers may do this by studying the research of academics, by learning to do ethnographic investigation themselves, or by teaching their students to research language and literacy practices in their own communities. Findings can then inform curriculum development in terms of selecting language of instruction, incorporating culturally familiar interactional patterns or genres into the curriculum, and/or drawing on content related to the heritage culture. The ultimate educational implication of social practices research is that it is important to hire teachers who come from the same cultural backgrounds as the learners because they are likely to be familiar with the learners' cultures, languages and literacy practices.

- *Supporting advocacy and informing policy*: finally, a commonly mentioned function of research on multilingual literacies is to inform and reform policy so that it is more reflective of real language and literacy uses. One such function is to support cultural maintenance or preservation: close description of previously unrecognized or unexamined literacy practices serves to affirm and validate local literacies and linguistic/cultural diversity, thus expanding the repertoire of what counts as 'acceptable' in a range of contexts. As such, the research can be a tool for resisting what has been called 'linguistic imperialism,' and informing advocacy for first language literacy instruction. Additionally, findings have enormous implications for designing family literacy programmes that support culture-specific home literacy practices (rather than simply transmitting school practices into the homes).

### Moving toward a critical approach to literacy research

A critical perspective on research is concerned with enacting changing power relations through the research process itself; as such, it asks questions like: who decides the research questions? Who engages in the research? Who produces knowledge, and who documents the knowledge that is produced? How is that knowledge used? On whose behalf? Who benefits from the research? And how does the research support or promote social change?

I would argue that in each of the above categories (domains, practices, roles, and functions), some applications of the socio-cultural paradigm could actually undermine a social justice agenda, others are irrelevant to it, and still others could contribute to it in concrete and useful ways. For example, if outside researchers utilize a socio-cultural perspective to document culture-specific literacy practices in a workplace domain for the purpose of retraining workers to produce more (and increase profits), this research could work against the workers' interests. If research is conducted to enhance a body of knowledge with no feedback to the subjects of the research, this, too, does nothing to change the circumstances of the subjects' lives. If research focuses closely on literacy practices of multilingual learners without considering problematic aspects of the context within which they take place, significant opportunities to act in concert with participants may be missed.

In what follows, I will look at each of the research categories in terms of its potential for shifting traditional power relations, deepening analysis of issues from the social context of participants' lives, and leading toward action. I am interested in those aspects of the paradigm that entail collaborative relationships that directly benefit non-academic participants, which position the research 'subjects' as active agents in the research process, and which support action for change in participants' lives. In short, I am interested in blurring the lines between research, pedagogy, and activism.

## Shifting traditional power relations

### Research functions

In a critical model, the function of literacy research shapes all other aspects of its implementation. Its most important function is one not usually mentioned in the socio-cultural paradigm, that of uncovering social issues in participants' social contexts and applying the research in service of addressing those issues. In a study of literacy practices among

Mexican Americans (Diaz, Moll and Mehan 1986: 211) designed to identify specific writing practices that could be incorporated into a high school curriculum, researchers found that: 'Virtually every conversation that began as a discussion of writing eventually turned to the problems of youth gangs, unemployment, immigration, the need to learn English and the like.' To me, this finding has enormously important implications: it suggests that literacy research can be a powerful tool in unearthing issues in community life. In classroom contexts as well, inviting students to research literacy practices can be a way in to discovering struggles in their lives. Pedagogical activities like asking students to do logs of language use or diaries about linguistically charged encounters, can at the same time, reveal interesting patterns or points of tension which can, in turn, become content for the curriculum.

### Research domains

In a critical model, domains could be classrooms or sites of community, workplace, or educational struggle. Organizations like unions, tenant rights groups, or other contexts in which community members address injustices might incorporate language/literacy research with the support of researchers or educators, recontextualizing literacy pedagogy so that sites of struggle become sites of learning. For example, the Right Question Project in Boston (2000) (www.rightquestion.org/) aims to teach immigrant parents to research question formulation in a variety of contexts so that parents can then ask 'the right questions' in advocating for their children, and challenging inequitable educational policies.

### Research roles

A critical model stresses repositioning those who are most often researched. Participants in the domains mentioned above may identify a concern that affects them and decide to investigate practices related to that concern. In this model, bilingual/ESOL students, community members, teachers and researchers collaborate with each other, transferring the tools of producing knowledge from those in dominant institutions to those in organizations on the ground (Rivera 1999).

### Research practices

Research practices in this model could be invoked either for the purpose of uncovering critical issues or to investigate issues and develop skills to address the issues. If the research context were classrooms, the focus would be on domains in students' lives where they experience conflict or struggle. Students would use ethnographic research tools (participant observation, interviews, inventories, surveys, diaries, photography, and so on) to look at literacy usage in these domains; in the process, however, it is likely that the research would contribute to deeper analysis of the issues (who is involved, how they interact, why, what are the power relationships and how do they shape interactions, and so on). Photography of community literacy artefacts or community mapping might, for example, reveal issues related to language or literacy discrimination, which in turn, may lead to analysis of power relations, and advocacy (for example, demands for translators, protests against language policies in welfare offices).

An example of this approach can be found in the *Action-Learning Manual* (Dixon and Cohen 1996), which contains seven activities that teach participants to research practices in their own communities for the purpose of identifying action projects. They connect researching family documents and photos, health records, agricultural and environmental records to raising awareness, developing literacy skills, and organizing around issues related to schooling, health and the environment.

The kind of research that I have described moves socio-cultural literacy research toward the well-established model of participatory action research model, a research paradigm which has a strong presence in other disciplines that also concern themselves with multilingual communities. In public health, for example, questions about power relations and community action are increasingly integrated into research methodologies (Minkler and Wallerstein 2003). Studies such as one entitled Participatory Action Research with Hotel Room Cleaners: A Case Study of First Steps in a Policy Change Campaign Guided by Community Based Participatory Research (Lee, Krause and Goetchius 2003) and another, entitled Using Photovoice as a Participatory Assessment and Issue Selection Tool (Wang 2003), teach community participants to use research practices not unlike those utilized in socio-cultural literacy research (for example, surveys, community mapping, photography, participant observation) for the purpose of documenting and acting on issues that impact their lives. In other words, these are projects that actually transfer the 'tools of production' of literacy research to community members, contributing to their ability to take action on their own behalves to challenge the structures and institutions that oppress them.

## Situating literacy research within a larger context

I want to end with two anecdotes and a question. The anecdotes come from colleagues whose literacy research initiatives, tragically, turned out quite differently than they had hoped. The first is from a colleague in Canada's Far North who participated in a literacy institute in which she shared a case study about a First Nations woman. The case study documented the literacy practices of this woman as she dealt with institutional bureaucracies including the medical system. After the institute was over, the researcher wrote to say that the woman, who had had a blood clot in her leg, went to the emergency room on numerous occasions with persistent breathlessness and coughing. On one occasion, she was told that the blood clot was gone and was sent home with cough medicine. She died a few days later. The second comes from colleagues who were researching the literacy and ESOL needs of asylum seekers in England. One of the subjects of the study was a young man from Afghanistan who was experiencing difficulties and alienation in adjusting to life in his new community. A footnote on the research report noted that this young man had committed suicide.

For these two individuals, it is impossible to separate out literacy practices from the dynamics of racism, exclusion, marginalization, and xenophobia within which they were embedded. The facts that a First Nations woman was given inadequate attention in an emergency room, and that an Afghani youth was forced to seek asylum in an unwelcoming, alienating environment are rooted in long-term historical relationships, militarization, and economic forces within communities impoverished by globalization. Their lives were shaped on the most basic level by transnational forces which are consolidating power and wealth in the hands of the few while increasing the impoverishment of the many. The reality of globalization is that, for example, 51 of the 100 largest economies in the world are corporations not countries; $1.5 trillion flows *daily* across international borders; there is a global assembly line linking the north and south with sweatshops, child labour, and the maquilladora system; transnational financial institutions such as the IMF and the World Bank supersede national governments; there is increasing privatization and deregulation of utilities, transport, and even water; welfare and government aid are being dismantled. All this is resulting in accelerating migration, increased concentration of wealth, growth of poverty, global ecological and environmental damage, and the decimation of human rights (Brecher, Costello and Smith 2000). While this reality is often not immediately visible through an ethnographic lens, I would argue that it contextualizes virtually every aspect of literacy research in multilingual communities; focusing primarily on the situational or institutional contexts within which literacy practices are enacted can obscure these larger geo-political dynamics which, in my view should be a starting point for critical literacy research.

What I am suggesting is an approach to research which puts itself in service of furthering struggles informed by a 'think globally, act locally' ideology. This argument is really old news in many parts of the world; Martin and Rahman (2001), for example, write about the lessons that those in the north can learn from literacy work in Bangladesh, saying: 'Learning is a process of political struggle, and education is an instrument to be used in this struggle' (p. 125). They argue in favour of what they call 'really useful literacy' which entails, among other things, 'acquiring practical knowledge to help people act on their world; ... harnessing learning to a social purpose; ... ensuring democratic control over the curriculum and the development of literacy materials; ... addressing gender inequities; ... respecting but also trusting the people' (pp. 122–5). They conclude by saying: 'One of the political lessons of globalization is that the local and specific struggles of ordinary people all over the world can become part of the wider, international struggle for democracy, social justice and equality. ... The question is: How can we make our work part of an alternative and deeply subversive "globalization from below"?' (p. 130).

The question that I would like to end with is: how can we take these principles, articulated in terms of literacy pedagogy, and begin to apply them as well to literacy research?

# References

Anderson, J., Kendrick, M., Rogers, T. and Smythe, S. (eds) (2005) *Portraits of Literacy Across Families, Communities, and Schools: Inter-sections and Tensions*. Mahwah, NJ: Lawrence Erlbaum Associates Inc.

Brecher, J., Costello, T. and Smith, B. (2000) *Globalization from Below: The Power of Solidarity*. Cambridge, MA: South End Press.

Diaz, S., Moll, L. and Mehan, H. (1986) 'Sociocultural resources in instruction: a context-specific approach' in Cortes, C.E. and California Office of Bilingual Education (eds) *Beyond Language: Social and Cultural Factors in Schooling Language Minority Students*. Los Angeles: California State University, Evaluation, Dissemination, and Assessment Center.

Dixon, J. and Cohen, J. (1996) *Literacy and Learning in Families and Communities Action Learning Manual: A Guide for Literacy Practitioners*. Amherst, MA: Center for International Education. Also download-able from www.cie@educ.umass.edu (accessed 2 July 2005).

Gee, J. (1996) *Social Linguistics and Literacies: Ideology in Discourses*, 2nd edn. London: Falmer Press.

Goldstein, T. (1997) *Two Languages at Work: Bilingual Life on the Production Floor*. New York: Mouton de Gruyter.

Gregory, E. (1998) 'Siblings as mediators of literacy in linguistic minority households'. *Language and Education*, 12(1): 33–54.

Heath, S.B. (1983) *Ways with Words*. Cambridge: Cambridge University Press.

Klassen, C. (1991) 'Bilingual written language use by low-education Latin American newcomers' in Barton, D. and Ivanic, R. (eds) *Writing in the Community*. London: Sage.

Lee, P., Krause, N. and Goetchius, C. (2003) 'Participatory action research with hotel room cleaners: from collaborative study to the bargaining table' in Minkler, M. and Wallerstein, N. (eds) *Community-Based Participatory Research for Health*. San Francisco: Jossey Bass.

Martin, I. and Rahman, H. (2001) 'The politics of really useful literacy: six lessons from Bangladesh' in Crowther, J., Hamilton, M. and Tett, L. (eds) *Powerful Literacies*. Leicester: NIACE.

Martin-Jones, M. and Jones, K. (eds) (2000) *Multilingual Literacies*. Amsterdam and Philadelphia, PA: John Benjamins.

Minkler, M. and Wallerstein, N. (eds) (2003) *Community-Based Participatory Research for Health*. San Francisco: Jossey Bass.

Moll, L. (1992) 'Literacy research in community and classrooms: a sociolcultural approach' in Beach, R., Green, J., Kamil, M. and Shanahan, T. (eds) *Multidisciplinary Perspectives on Literacy Research*. Urbana, IL: National Council of Teachers of English.

Right Question Project in Boston (2000) downloadable from www.rightquestion.org/ (accessed 21 April 2005).

Rivera, K. (1999) 'Popular research and social transformation: a community-based approach to critical pedagogy'. *TESOL Quarterly*, 33(3): 485–500.

Roberts, C., Byram, M., Barro, A, Jordan, S. and Street, B. (2001) *Language Learners as Ethnographers*. Clevedon: Multilingual Matters.

Rockhill, K. (1993) 'Gender, language and the politics of literacy' in Street, B. (ed.) *Cross-Cultural Approaches to Literacy*. Cambridge: Cambridge University Press.

Scribner, S. and Cole, M. (1981) *The Psychology of Literacy*. Cambridge, MA: Harvard University Press.

Stein, S. (1997) *Equipped for the Future: A Reform Agenda for Adult Literacy and Lifelong Learning*. Washington, DC: National Institute for Literacy.

Street, B. (1984) *Literacy in Theory and Practice*. Cambridge: Cambridge University Press.

Street, B. (1996) 'Preface: the social uses of literacy' in Prinsloo, M. and Breier, M. (eds) *Theory and Practice in Contemporary South Africa*. Cape Town and Amsterdam: SACHED Books and John Benjamins.

Wang, C. (2003) 'Using photovoice as a participatory assessment and issue selection tool' in Minkler, M. and Wallerstein, N. (eds) *Community-Based Participatory Research for Health*. San Francisco: Jossey Bass.

# 6 Language, Literacy and Bilingualism: Connecting Theory, Policy and Practice

*Celia Roberts*

## Introduction

A 'bilingual' student, in this chapter, refers to anyone from a linguistic minority who has some ability in a second language, in this context, English. Every bilingual varies in their ability in and use of the second language (Romaine 1995) and this is one of the reasons why policy and provision for adult bilingual learners has had such a chequered history. The contested definition of what 'bilingualism' means is also reflected in the different labels given to learners of English. In selecting 'ESOL', I am using the current UK Department for Education and Skills label in order to avoid being mired in a long (if interesting) debate about definitions. However, the fact that there is the need for this paragraph is indicative of much of the discussion below about where language learning theory, policy and practice fit with adult literacy and numeracy.

Policymakers have, traditionally, been rather uncomfortable with where to place linguistic minority learners when dealing with literacy, numeracy and language development. This has been for three main reasons. First, there is the continued tension between separating out such learners from other basic skills provision and so being open to the charge of marginalizing and ghettoizing the group or, conversely, treating linguistic minorities as part of the mainstream and so making them invisible.

A cursory glance at government documents shows this tension with language mentioned alongside literacy and numeracy sometimes, but not always, and ESOL added to literacy and numeracy with the same kind of frequency. The position of ESOL in the National Research and Development Centre for Adult Literacy and Numeracy is a further example of this tension. The same tensions are reported in the other English dominant countries. In North America, Australia and New Zealand, it has been common practice to conflate language and literacy (Davison 1996, in Murray 2005: 67) and so the distinction between first and second language development can be blurred or even lost (Murray 2005).

Second, as the opening paragraph above suggests, the discourses of language, minorities, ethnicity, culture and so on are contested. Often these discourses are stigmatizing, inaccurate or theoretically complex. Policy writers want simple categories. For example, in Leung, Harris and Rampton (1997) the terms 'mother tongue' and 'native speaker' are challenged. Instead the terms 'language expertise', 'language inheritance' and 'language affiliation' are proposed.

Third, the ideologies and heterogeneous goals of ESOL provision and ESOL learners can make for differences between policy agendas and learners' goals (Auerbach 1985). The diversity of learners from highly skilled professionals to those who have no functional literacy in their heritage language is subsumed under the all too elastic notion of ESOL. Simple functional skills for 'getting by' contrast with long-term agendas of acquiring extensive linguistic knowledge for future academic courses and these in turn are different from the complex discursive and cultural practices that fluent, but recently arrived, professional migrants or refugees may need. Policymakers, teachers and learners may all relate to these different ideologies and goals in different ways. For example, in the 1980s and 1990s functional ESOL courses were criticized by some teachers for positioning learners as 'needy'; or, for example, some learners want more grammar either because this is what they are familiar with and can talk about or because it is a way of resisting the socio-cultural content of the course and its requirements to be socially appropriate and acceptable to the white majority group (Canagarajah 2001).

A socio-cultural, situated learning approach to language and literacy also has to wrestle with these issues. And relating theory to policy is particularly difficult where, on the one hand, policy is concerned with goals and outcomes and these theories, on the other, with processes. More generally, language provision for linguistic minorities has been under-theorized compared with work in second language acquisition (SLA). This is largely because of the lack, until very recently, of nationally coordinated research on linguistic minorities in most English-speaking countries except for Australia and, to some extent, Canada.

## Language socialization within structural relations of inequality

Language use and development within a basic skills frame are no more neutral skills than literacy:

> I prefer to work from what I term the 'ideological model of language and literacy', that recognizes a multiplicity of language

uses and literacies; that the meaning and uses of language and literacy practices are related to specific cultural contexts; and that these practices are always associated with relations of power and ideology, they are not simply neutral technologies. (Street 1984: 139)

This socio-cultural situated practice theory of literacy is also a theory of language use, discourse and social identity. In terms of language development, it links with theories of second language socialization (SLS) (as opposed to second language acquisition) (Zuengler and Cole 2005). Like the theories of situated literacy, SLS is a social theory in which meaning making, and what counts as meaning, is always related to specific contexts. SLS involves both the necessary socialization to use language and the process of socialization through language (Ochs and Schieffelin 1983). In other words, learners have to understand the behaviours, values and practices of a community in order to use language. And in using language they come to learn these ways of being and doing. Since SLS takes place in, typically, stratified multilingual societies, the process is always concerned with relations of power and ideology. The immediate context, reflected in and created by interaction, feeds into the wider social context of inequality. For example, interaction positions people and provides the evidence for judging them. In intercultural encounters, differences and misunderstandings feed into widely held linguistic ideologies about English, what constitutes 'a native language speaker' and so on. In contrast with literacy practices among those whose dominant language is English, second language and literacy practices are much more likely to be developed in formal or institutional settings where relations of power are more palpable. For all these reasons, any policy and practice related to language and literacy for linguistic minorities needs to focus also on the whole communicative environment within which they learn and acknowledge the (potential) discrimination which is a part of it (Zuengler and Cole 2005).

In SLS, language and culture are 'wired in together' (Agar 1994). For example, in a typical institutionalized encounter such as a job-counselling interview, successful discourse strategies include more than the grammar and pragmatics of many ESOL courses. Such strategies include an understanding of: expectations about specific goals (actions), speaker rights and responsibilities (social identities), some level of agreement about the boundaries of what constitutes the personal (cultural knowledge), and some understanding of how indirectness is used in social categorization (face and stance). An ability to process the linguistic code, including intonation and other aspects of prosody, and draw inferences from it about the kind of socio-cultural knowledge and contexts just described needs to be part of a core curriculum. Such interpretive strategies are not developed easily or on short courses but require long exposure to communicative experiences in networks of relationship (Gumperz 1996). This wiring in of language and culture is just as important in embedded teaching and learning where language and vocational skills are integrated. For example, on a course for overseas nurses, the professional and institutional discourses required for being a nurse in the NHS link social knowledge and stance with the pragmatic skills of persuading and empathizing (Shrubshall and Roberts forthcoming).

Like the new literacy studies, SLS studies also rely on ethnographic method to understand the lived experiences of linguistic minorities in a more holistic way. Ethnographic method contributes to an understanding of how linguistic minorities are positioned in intercultural encounters and the long-term effects of this on individual motivation, personal and social investment and the construction of social identities (Pierce 1995). It also contributes to an understanding of language and literacy uses outside these institutional encounters, and to descriptions of resources in languages and literacies which are often invisible to the institutional agencies that develop and implement policy.

## Skills for Life policy and the Adult Literacy and Numeracy Initiative from a linguistic minority learner perspective

There is a danger in getting mired in mutual criticism when we look at the relationship between theory, policy and practice. From the perspective of any of them, the other two seem wanting. So, although there are some negative critiques in this chapter, it is important to recognize how policy, theory and practice are in their different ways affording opportunities and helping us to understand and evaluate them. The *Review of Adult ESOL Pedagogy Research* (Barton and Pitt 2003) gives an overview of research which includes research on policy, provision and practically relevant research as well as more theoretically driven studies.

There is the potential for these three elements to inform each other. For example, SLS theory combined with the kind of interpretive research which aims to understand the whole context in which second language learning takes place and not just look for quick technical solutions (what Bloor calls enlightenment rather than engineering research, Bloor 1997) both informs, and is informed by, provision. The workplace case study below illustrates an approach to workplace learning where the whole communicative context of the workplace is accounted for in the development of language education programmes. Similarly, the case for embedded language learning, mentioned above, is strengthened by SLS and interpretive case study research which sheds light on how the vocational context provides opportunities for learning the socio-cultural knowledge that is wired into language use.

However, current English national policy, despite the general 'social inclusion' framing of social policy generally, does not deal explicitly with issues of language and cultural practice within the wider context of structural inequality. The institutionalized frameworks within which skills for life are 'delivered' are treated as culturally neutral. For example:

- *'Boosting demand'*: there is an underlying discourse concerning individual motivation and confidence, supported by networks but little explicit recognition that some groups and individuals meet active resistance at home to the chance of learning (Alam 2000). The goal of 'boosting demand' has to be sensitive to this issue.
- *'Building capacity'* in teacher training and other forms of networking. For example, in the subject specification for ESOL teachers, there is: very little on culturally different styles of learning and communicating and how learners can adapt to the different classroom cultures that emerge; relatively little on making explicit the interpretive rules of institutional interaction; little on recognizing the existing language and literacy resources of learners.
- *Strategies for capacity building* do not reflect lessons learned from multi- and bilingual literacy projects where bi/multilingual staff's own development has been part of the project and where progression to further community provision is built in (Gurnah 2000).
- *'Standards'*: there is a need for provision and curricular policy which takes account of issues of length and intensity necessary for second language socialization and for creating learning environments outside the classroom. International comparisons show great variety in terms of number of hours considered adequate to move from beginner to having simple functional competence (see Murray 2005).
- *'Achievement'*: it is assumed that individual learning plans (ILPs) are relevant and appropriate for ESOL classes where often larger numbers and more whole class and group work make ILPs less relevant. The complexity of the curriculum also makes it harder for those with limited English to engage in the process of

planning their own learning. And ILPs tend to be framed in terms of individual, cognitive goals rather than social and interactional ones. Yet programmes are evaluated on the basis that ILPs are necessary and effective (Ofsted 2003). The heterogeneity of many ESOL classes, the problems of negotiating learning plans when there is no common language to do this and the assumption, challenged by language-learning theorists, that language development is like putting the pieces of a jigsaw together, all make for difficulties with ILPs in ESOL classes (Sunderland and Wilkins 2004).

## Workplace language and literacy for linguistic minorities: a brief case study

In order to ground these rather general issues in specific provision, I want to take a look at workplace provision. This is high on policy agendas as a result of the Moser report, and initiatives such as the Lancaster University Workplace Basic Skills Network and the Basic Skills Agency Brokerage Scheme mean that infrastructures are in place. Workplace basic skills development also has aspects in common with the embedded basic skills approach in which language, literacy and numeracy are embedded in vocational or recreational skills development (LSDA 2002). There are also lessons to be learnt from workplace language projects in Australia and North America, and from England in the 1970s and 1980s. Finally, the studies on the new work order have implications for language and literacy (Gee, Hull and Lankshear 1996). These studies show that because of more flexible working practices, more multitask working and flatter structures, there is more talk at work and more talk about talk (Iedema and Scheeres 2004).

The workplace offers situated language and literacy learning. To put it more strongly, 'the workplace is the curriculum' (Mawer 1999). All aspects of workplace life have the potential for developing language and literacy if the communicative environment is geared to learning. However, with a multilingual workforce, gearing up brokers, providers and union learning representatives to appreciate workplace language needs, although important, is not enough. Negative linguistic ideologies, the casual racism stemming from perceived differences and opportunities and difficulties created by cultural and linguistic diversity also have to be confronted. In particular, there is a widespread ideology that language programmes should gear up learners either to do their current job better or get any menial job, whereas most learners want to attend classes to get a better job (Tollefson 1991).

Ethnographic research and long-term projects based in companies have also shown that the goal of communicative competence is not the panacea for all the difficulties and inequalities in the workplace. Improving language skills does not necessarily offer learners promotion since most jobs require a higher general level of education. Needs analysis, language training and assessment can all marginalize and disadvantage linguistic minority learners since they can mask the situated competency of workers and ignore their overseas qualifications and communicative resources in other languages (Hull 1997; Mawer 1999). Rather than any narrow needs analysis, Australian research has shown the need for a wider communications audit which includes potential learners' own perspectives on language and literacy.

In many multilingual workplaces where a work group share a common minority language, the investment in that language as a means of social cohesion can be overlooked (Goldstein 1997). There are often gaps between the language and literacy skills needed for a job and the language and literacy required for training and assessment. This is linked to wider misperceptions about the language required for the job. Employers tend to overestimate the language requirements for many jobs and these judgements can then get fed into policy requirements about language levels (Schellekens 2001). Projects where language specialists have been attached to workplaces for an extended period have been able to tackle language misperceptions and ideologies as well as having an impact on a whole range of work practices such as setting competency standards, advising on training, on the design of new forms and so on (Mawer 1999).

There is always a tension between developing situated learning programmes based on workplace-perceived needs, and understanding from an insider perspective the complex motivations, constraints and positionings of those targeted as learners. This is true of homogeneous workforces as well as linguistically and ethnically heterogeneous ones. But is relatively harder to understand and act on in the case of the latter. What is important is that the workplace offers situated learning, provided that it is transformed into a learning environment that takes account of learners' perceived needs and not just those of the workplace.

## Conclusion

I have argued here for a research and policy agenda which challenges traditional ideas about language learning as acquisition of the linguistic code (SLA). A model of second language socialization helps to redefine the goals of language learning and the methods to realize them. It also informs the debate about length of provision and provides evidence of the complexity of the task of participating fully in a community of practice. Since people are learning English in multilingual environments the simple apprenticeship model of gradually being inducted into some stable language practices is no longer adequate. Policy and practice also have to take account of how learners can be socialized into communities where varieties of English are spoken.

One of the most striking aspects of policy in multilingual societies is the separation of race/ethnicity issues, cultural processes and language. Policy in this area needs an overarching framework which incorporates the wider social context of inequality. Within this wider context, these three issues are profoundly interconnected. Such a framework would inform, at least, the following areas:

- Explicit recognition of bi/multilingual resources in building capacity, developing provision.
- Debating how learners are to be categorized and the effect this has on provision for example, EFL, ESOL, mainstream and so on, and the importance of an insider/learner perspective (from ethnographic studies) in categorizing learners.
- Explicit recognition of situated learning in clear progression routes for learners.
- Acknowledging achievement in multilingual contexts for example, assessment that takes account of learners' competence and use of more than one language in contexts of use.
- Clearer acknowledgement of the ESOL classroom as a place where different cultures of learning emerge – where tensions are managed between experience-based, progressive and celebratory practices, on the one hand, and rigorous, systematic, language knowledge-based practices, on the other – and even where self-expression is a key practice, acknowledge that learners do not necessarily wish to present only the identity of themselves as 'immigrants', 'newcomers' and so on (Roberts et al. 2004).
- Acknowledgement that workplace, embedded and other courses, where the boundary between the classroom and beyond is crossed, can provide opportunities but that these are not neutral environments. They offer chances but only where the communicative environment is sensitive to the lived experiences of learners.

# References

Agar, M. (1994) *Language Shock*. New York: William Morrow.

Alam, Y. (2000) 'Gender, literacy and community publishing in a multilingual context', in Martin-Jones, M. and Jones, K. (eds) *Multilingual Literacies*. Philadelphia, PA: John Benjamins.

Auerbach, E. (1985) 'The hidden curriculum of survival ESL'. *TESOL Quarterly*, 19: 475–94.

Barton, D. and Pitt, K. (2003) *Adult ESOL Pedagogy*. London: National Research and Development Centre for Adult Literacy and Numeracy.

Bloor, M. (1997) 'Addressing social problems through qualitative research' in Silverman, D. (ed.) *Qualitative Research: Theory, Method and Practice*. London: Sage.

Canagarajah, S. (2001) 'Critical ethnography of a Sri Lankan classroom' in Candlin, C.N. and Mercer, N. (eds) *English Language Teaching in its Social Context*. London: Open University Press, Macquarie University and Routledge.

Duff, P. (1996) 'Different languages, different practices: socialisation of discourse competence in dual-language school classrooms in Hungary' in Bailey, K. and Nunan, D. (eds) *Voices from the Language Classroom: Qualitative Research in Second Language Education Research*. New York: Cambridge University Press.

Gee, J., Hull, G. and Lankshear, C. (1996) *The New Work Order: Behind the Language of the New Capitalism*. Sydney: Allen & Unwin.

Goldstein, T. (1997) *Two Languages at Work: Bilingual Life on the Production Floor*. Berlin: Mouton de Gruyter.

Gumperz, J. (1996) 'The linguistic and cultural relativity of conversational inference' in Gumperz, J. and Levinson, S. (eds) *Rethinking Linguistic Relativity*. Cambridge: Cambridge University Press.

Gurnah, A. (2000) 'Languages and literacies for autonomy' in Martin-Jones, M. and Jones, K. (eds) *Multilingual Literacies*. Philadelphia: John Benjamins.

Hull, G. (ed.) (1997) *Changing Work, Changing Workers: Critical Perspectives on Language, Literacy and Skills*. Albany, NY: State University of New York Press.

Iedema, R. and Scheeres, H. (2004) 'From doing work to talking work: renegotiating knowing, doing and identity'. *Special issue of Applied Linguistics*.

Learning Skills Development Agency (2002) *Evaluation of Basic Skills and ESOL in Local Community Projects*. London: LSDA.

Leung, C., Harris, R. and Rampton, B. (1997) 'The idealized native speaker, reified ethnicities and classroom realities'. *TESOL Quarterly*, 31: 543–60.

Martin-Jones, M. and Jones, K. (eds) (2000) *Multilingual Literacies.* Philadelphia, PA: John Benjamins.

Mawer, G. (1999) *Language and Literacy in Workplace Education: Learning at Work.* London: Longman.

Murray, D. (2005) 'ESL in adult education' in Hinkel, E. (ed.) *Handbook of Research in Second Language Learning and Teaching.* Mahwah, NJ: Lawrence Erlbaum Associates Inc.

Ochs, E. and Schieffelin, B. (1983) *Acquiring Conversational Competence.* Boston, MA: Routledge & Kegan Paul.

Ofsted (2003) *Literacy, Numeracy and English for Speakers of Other Languages: A Survey of Current Practice in Post-16 and Adult Provision.* London: DfES.

Pierce, B. (1995) 'Social identity, investment and language learning'. *TESOL Quarterly,* 29: 9–31.

Romaine, S. (1995) *Bilingualism.* Boston, MA: Basil Blackwell.

Roberts, C., Baynham, M., Shrubshall, P., Barton, D., Chopra, P., Cooke, M., Hodge, R., Pitt, K., Schellekens, P., Wallace, C. and Whitfield, S. (2004) *English for Speakers of Other Languages (ESOL) Case Studies of Provision, Learners' Needs and Resources.* London: National Research and Development Centre.

Schellekens, P. (2001) *English Language as a Barrier to Employment, Training and Education.* London: DfEE.

Shrubshall, P. and Roberts, C. (forthcoming) 'Being a nurse and following new rules: professional and institutional discourses in a preparatory course for supervized practice for overseas nurses' in Roberts, C., Baynham, M., Shrubshall, P., Brittan, J., Cooper, B., Gidley, N., Windsor, V., Eldred, J., Grief, S., Castillino, C. and Walsh, M. (eds) *Embedded Skills – Case Studies.* London: National Research and Development Centre for Adult Literacy and Numeracy.

Street, B. (1984) *Literacy in Theory and Practice.* Cambridge: Cambridge University Press.

Sunderland, H. and Wilkins, M. (2004) 'ILPS in ESOL: theory, research and practice'. *Reflect,* 1: 8–9. London National Research and Development Centre for Adult Literacy and Numeracy.

Tollefson, J. (1991) *Planning Language, Planning Inequality: Language Policy in the Community.* London: Longman.

Zuengler, J. and Cole, K. (2005) 'Language socialization and second language learning', in Hinkel, E. (ed.) *Handbook of Research on Second Language Teaching and Learning.* Mahwah, NJ: Lawrence Erlbaum Associates Inc.

# 7 Literacy, Language and Bilingualism

*Mahendra Verma*

In this chapter, I shall try to give a brief resumé of the limited research available in the area of literacy, language and bilingualism from a grassroots' perspective.

Linguistic diversity in transplanted, diaspora and marginalized communities is at the interface of bilingualism and biliteracy. The language and literacy experience or lack of it in the ethnic minority communities settled in the UK's multilingual and multicultural settings is enormously rich for some but poor for others. One recognizes the significance of reading and writing in different orthographic traditions as social practices, very different from academic practices. Many ethnographic researchers (Street 1984) have realized that there are different literacy practices in different cultures. In our pilot survey of adult South Asians at several ESOL centres (Khanna, et al. 1998) we found that on the basis of literacy practices and literacy competencies one could group the ethnic minority adult learners into three categories:

1  those who have had their education in the subcontinent and were bi- and multiliterate, for example: Hindi, Urdu and English or Hindi, Panjabi and English or Hindi, Panjabi, Urdu and English or Hindi and English
2  those who were literate in Hindi or Bangla or Gujerati or Gurmukhi Panjabi only
3  those who did not have the opportunity to go to school and become literate or acquire literacy at home, for example many rural-based migrants from Sylhet in Bangladesh.

In our visits to their homes, the examples of visual literacy items, for example books, magazines, newspapers, varied from 'quite visible' to 'marginally visible' or almost non-existent. The literacy practices loosely corresponded to the 'visibility' situation. It is mainly because 'literacy practices' are sometimes shared by the community. A friend or family member competent in literacy in the heritage language would act as an aide, and write letters and read letters on behalf of some members of the community. This community spirit has been transported from the rural South Asian countries to the highly literacy-dependent culture of industrialized Britain. My focus in this chapter will be on the literacy practices and literacy events in the South Asian communities with special reference to one vibrant and dynamic literacy and oracy event, that is: literary events.

The situation with regard to bilingualism and literacy practices in England projects an ecological picture which, on the one hand, officially defines and promotes adult literacy as literacy in English only, and which, on the other, aspires for and promotes bi/multiliteracy practices without any official help and support.

Many South Asian adults, though not all, aspire to connect themselves fully with the real world of literacy: functional, cultural, and critical. Functional literacy is often related to basic skills in writing and reading, which allow people to produce and understand useful messages in notes, posters, advertisements or notices. Native or heritage language literacy is inextricably associated with the past and also with the contemporary cultural experiences. Cultural literacy's focus, by way of contrast, is on the need for shared new experiences and inherited experiences of the past reflected in the heritage language texts which need to be fully comprehensible to people across generations. Critical literacy identifies the political and ideological message inherent in heritage language reading and writing. The ethnic newspapers published in the UK as well as those that come from the subcontinent are good examples. To be 'literate' and to be an active participant in the heritage language literacy practices means to be able to appreciate the content of the text. This encourages us to introduce the notion of literary or creative literacy. The indentured Bhojpuri Hindi labourers who were transplanted by the British Raj in Mauritius used the rocks and stones to give Devanagari literacy lessons to their illiterate friends so that the rich religious and non-religious literary texts could be preserved and successive generations helped to inherit them. The urge to transmit their culture was so strong that they assembled in secrecy to take part in this exercise.

In the UK, composing and reciting new and traditional folk songs is closely associated with South Asian cultural activities, including weddings and religious events. The ritual popularly known as 'akhaND paaTh' in the Hindu community, which involves reading and reciting from the holy book *The Ramcharitmanas* (popularly called the *Ramayan*) over a period precisely of 24 hours is an event which takes place either at an individual's house or in a temple. The Sikhs, too, read their own holy book (the *Guru Granth Sahib*) as part of the 'akhaND paaTh'. Special songs sung on the occasion of weddings, births and deaths and the recitation of the holy book are dependent on either literacy competence or on memory. In my ethnographic research, I found that generally the older adults (40+) have both oracy and literacy competence, but it is not being transmitted to the younger adults. The younger adults and children are extending their literacy in English to these texts. There is also the tradition of singing hymns from a hymnbook or from memory. These texts are transliterated for them in Roman for reading and recitation purposes in the temple.

Writing short stories, novels and poetry in the heritage languages is cathartic for writers who have a lot to say about their community's varied diaspora experiences, including that of marginalization and discrimination. This literary literacy tradition largely goes unnoticed by the majority community in which creativity in English alone is legitimized and recognized. In our research on adult ESOL learners in Britain (Khanna et al. 1998) we found that in the majority of the centres the curriculum and pedagogical practices did not reflect the lived and living experiences of the learners.

In an environment of ideological conflict between the supremacy of English literacy promoting mono-literacy and the sustenance and development of heritage language literacy promoting multiliteracy, empirical data, although very scant, suggest that there is widespread lack of motivation among some groups of bilingual adults regarding acquiring literacy in their heritage languages. However, the desire and the aspiration to transmit it to the younger generation are generally there. In his study of the home literacy practices of 18 Sylheti-speaking Bangladeshi women in Birmingham, Blackledge reported that they 'felt marginalized by the school's day-to-day ideology of English as the sole language of communication in and about school' (Blackledge 2000: 36). These women claimed proficiency in reading and writing in Bangla, which they were trying to transmit to their children. However, 'despite their literacies, the women's lack of English proficiency led the teachers to position them as illiterate' (Blackledge 2000: 37). In my study of the Bangladeshi older and younger adults who had missed out on education in Bangladesh, it was clear that, although they wanted their children to acquire oracy and literacy in Bangla, they themselves were very reluctant to register for heritage language literacy classes. In her study of the place of literacies in the lives of a dozen or so Pakistani Muslim women in Brierfield, Hartley (1994) observed

> [T]he apparent lack of need for reading and writing in the everyday lives of some women. In particular in the lives of many older women who had not had the opportunity of schooling seemed structured in such a way that literacy skills ... appeared

of minor importance. Brought up with a wealth of oral tradition, these women had an apparently inexhaustible fund of children's stories, songs, family histories, descriptions and instructions stored in their minds – without my constant need for a written aide-memoir! (Hartley 1994: 32).

In his research on bilingualism and literacy practices among the Panjabi Hindus in Southall, Saxena (1994) made an in-depth ethnographic study of one three-generational family's complex and variable literacy repertoire and literacy practices. The grandfather, educated in India, had brought with him competencies in various literacies for example, Devanagari Hindi, Gurmukhi Panjabi, Urdu and English, which in the course of the day he practised appropriately on different occasions at different places in Southall. The grandmother raised in Kenya, with no formal education, had acquired adequate literacy in Hindi, which enabled her to read and write letters received from India. She also read Hindi newspapers and magazines in the temple library. She read bilingual English–Hindi notices displayed on shop windows. She read Hindi letters and newspapers at home to her son, who was educated in the UK, and had literacy competence in English only. Her daughter-in-law, educated in India, had good competence in Hindi language and literacy. In her leisure time she read Hindi novels, and shared the reading of Hindi letters from India. Whenever she brought a letter from their child's nursery written in English, her husband read it out and explained to her. Their son is growing up observing the multiliteracy practices in the family. In my own study of the Hindi-speaking families, I found that in the first generation, Hindi–English biliteracy is quite common among those who were educated in India. They often read Hindi letters to their children. It is quite common to find ingredients and dosage printed in Hindi, Urdu, Panjabi, Bangla and Gujerati on spice and pickle jars and on herbal medicines. However, quite a large number of the second and the third generation educated in the UK have not had the opportunity or the instrumental or integrative motivation to acquire biliteracy. The older and the younger generations have different oracy and literacy backgrounds. Although many of the members of the older generation have bilingualism and biliteracy, in certain contexts for example, talking about recipes the oral tradition continues. The grandmothers are not used to cooking or talking about food based on written recipes whereas the grandchildren growing up in the print culture of English orthography, literacy alien to the grandmother, have neither acquired the oral tradition nor the literacy tradition or practices in the heritage language. Mono-literacy is what they have inherited from the English tradition.

Although linguistic diversity, including multiculturalism, has been of growing concern to many working with young children it is increasingly becoming evident that we have ignored a holistic approach, which would have helped us recognize the interrelationships that exist between the child and the adult in the family and the community. The typical approach to and focus of research in ESOL acquisition has been on all the four skills in English and English alone.

The writing process which involves 'construction' (pre-writing stage of selection of meanings), 'execution' (actual physical process of producing the text, hand written or word processed) and 'transformation' (composition and revision) also relies on the feedback from the 'reading' and the 'listening' audience. There has been a steady growth of creative writing in the first-generation South Asians. South Asian community supported by numerous literary bodies, for example: UK Hindi Samiti (UK Hindi Society), London; Gitanjali Multilingual Literary Circle, Birmingham; Bhartiya Bhasha Sangam (Indian Languages Association, York); Mini Mushaira (Mini-Poetry Recitation, Sheffield), Katha (UK). These literary groups organize national and international kavi sammelans and mushairas (poets' assembly) and katha (short story) workshops at which poets and short story writers read their creative writings, and they get instant feedback from the large audience. Although the participants' age ranges from 25 to 70, it is the older generation that dominates the number. The audience attendance at poetry festival runs into hundreds. These evening performances are lively and dynamic like pop concerts, and often last longer than the scheduled programmes. Over a period of the last five years my research survey of the participants in these literary festivals found that the majority of the audience belonged to the older first generation, which included both the elite and non-elite classes. Chatterjee (2002) herself a Bengali poet talking about mushaira said:

> Mushaira is nothing if not socially inclusive. The fact that it is free and is perceived to be an enjoyable sociable occasion means that it can command a large audience from all walks of life. Attending a mushaira does not carry the stigma that many British poetry readings do – of being a highbrow activity. (Chatterjee 2002: 75)

My interviews with the second and third generations suggested that since they did not have literacy competence in the heritage language they felt completely cut off from this part of their cultural heritage. In October 2005 the BBC launched its digital radio Asian Network. Not surprisingly, it set out its aims as: 'The Asian Network is aimed at second and third generation Asians, and broadcasts a mix of speech and music.

... While most of the output is in English, programmes in Hindi–Urdu, Mirpuri, Gujarati, Bengali and Panjabi will feature at night.' This process and ideology of implicit and induced 'divorce' from the linguistic, literary and literacy tradition is another step in that direction. Some of the older adults who enjoyed participating in these literary activities felt they would have understood the culturally embedded nuances of meaning better if they had the literacy skills to read the printed literary texts. Dominic Rai (Artistic Director of the British–Panjabi theatre company Man Mela) has said:

> Panjabi is the second most widely spoken language in England. There are many thousands of people who speak it every day but who don't necessarily know how to read and write ... the Gurmukhi. For that reason, it is important to translate their works into English in order to reach the widest possible audience and enable the Panjabi community to understand its cultural heritage. There is a massive audience out there. (Watts 2001: 9)

Translation has an important role to play in cross-linguistic and cross-cultural fertilization, but with the loss of the literacy tradition literacy practices in the heritage languages might gradually evaporate and with that the interest and motivation of the massive audience. In my interviews, it was evident that the massive audience would shrink if poetry readings were in English translation only.

## Conclusion

It is apparent that there has been a lack of national commitment to bi/ multiliteracy. In contrast to research on childhood bilingualism, the amount of in-depth empirical research on bilingual adult multiliteracy practices and the state support it gets is quite limited in this country. Daniel Weissbort, editor of *Modern Poetry in Translation* said:

> Poetry happens everywhere, but sometimes (often) it happens in languages which do not attract attention. We are the poorer for not experiencing it, at least to the extent that it can be experienced in translation. This is particularly immature, surely, when it is actually happening next door! (Weissbort 2001: 8)

Examining the progress adult and further education have made in contributing to the sustenance and or the development of biliteracy among minority adult bilinguals in the UK, one comes to the conclusion that this enterprise is only half on the agenda, the ESOL half; the other half, the heritage language half, is almost non-existent. Stephen Watts, guest editor of the poetry anthology *Mother Tongue* said: 'There is still in this country a striking ignorance as to the range and quality of non-English language poetries being written here' (Watts 2001: 11).

Watts hopes this ignorance will soon be overcome, and mainstream major British poets will 'become an obvious and natural part of reading circuits, however beautiful and sharp and radical a cultural shift that may require' (Watts 2001: 11).

The questions that should be on the minds of both the promoters of a multilingual and multiliterate society and those opposed to it are: would the rich oral folk tradition, which bilinguals in the diaspora community have brought from largely rural, oral societal tradition to a highly industrialized literate society in the UK, survive the second and third generation? Would the ecology of monoliteracy in England discourage the development of new diasporic literature in ethnic minority heritage languages in the second, third and subsequent generations? Would English literature be poorer without its interaction with other literary traditions? Would there be an audience in Britain equipped to read, and write poetry in Tamil, Somali or Urdu and appreciate the diasporic literature reflecting ethnic minority's emotions and feelings, tensions and struggles? If the minorities do not inherit and acquire the dynamic culture of reading and writing traditional and new diaspora-grown literatures in heritage languages, would bilingualism survive? Would bilingualism survive without biliteracy in a literacy-dominated western urban culture and society?

# References

Blackledge, A. (2000) 'Monolingual ideologies in multilingual states: language, hegemony and social justice in Western liberal democracies'. *Estudios de Sociolinguistica*, 1: 2.

Chatterjee, D. (2002) 'A little bridge' in Robinson, M. (ed.) *Words Out Loud*. Devon: Stride.

Hartley, T. (1994) 'Generations of literacy among women in a bilingual community' in Hamilton, M. Barton, D. and Ivanic, R. (eds) *Worlds of Literacy*. Clevedon: Multilingual Matters.

Khanna, A.L., Verma, M. and Chatterjee, D. (1998) *Adult ESOL Learners in Britain: A Cross-Cultural Study*. Clevedon: Multilingual Matters.

Saxena, M. (1994) 'Literacies among Panjabis in Southall' in Hamilton, M. Barton, D. and Ivanic, R. (eds) *Worlds of Literacy*. Clevedon: Multilingual Matters.

Street, B. (1984) *Literacy in Theory and Practice*. New York: Cambridge University Press.

Watts, S. (ed.) (2001) *Mother Tongues*. London: King's College.

Weissbort, D. (2001) 'To the reader' in Watts, S. (ed.) *Mother Tongues*. London: King's College.

# Section Three
## The Politics of Numbers

# 8    Power of Numbers: Research Agendas in a Number-saturated World

*Mike Baynham*

As a small boy of eight, new to an English boarding school, I experienced many dislocations and estrangements from my familiar world. Here I was typically addressed by my surname for example. Stranger still I was given a number, 103, which was my number in that it featured on my locker and on all my clothes which were marked with a name tag *M.J. Baynham 103*. I have not the slightest idea to what administrative system the number contributed, yet I must have been obscurely proud of having it. To this day, when I come across the number 103 in some everyday context, on a car number plate for example, I think of it as *my* number.

I would like to be able to say that this was my earliest exposure to the power and indeed the allure of numbers but this is, of course, not the case. I had been born into a number-saturated social world (if you want to engage the attention of a 4-year-old ask how old he or she is) and it is on this number-saturated social world that I will focus in this chapter. I took from this early experience and no doubt other experiences a lifelong interest in dislocation and estrangement and indeed with victims and victimization which has, I think, informed my research in different ways. I cannot however say that I developed a similar passion for understanding the role of numbers in social life, or certainly not until comparatively recently. So how was I invited to contribute a chapter on the power of numbers given that I am, if anything, a 'language and literacy person'? A further autobiographical digression is in order. My interest and involvement in adult numeracy started in the 1990s, when I was working at the University of Technology, Sydney (UTS) with an exciting grouping of adult language, literacy and numeracy colleagues, during the heady days of the ALLP (Australian Language and Literacy – yes, not numeracy, as I'll discuss later – Policy), where considerable funding was made available for innovative research and curriculum projects in Australia. My first funded research project was a classroom-based study investigating the role of language in adult numeracy classrooms (Baynham 1995, 1996).

At this time I also worked with colleagues in the maths department at UTS in a similar study, this time with an intended curriculum outcome, looking at the language demands of the first year of the undergraduate maths degree (Baynham, Wood and Smith 1995). Both of these studies involved what has been called 'the linguistic turn', the realization that linguistic analysis is a powerful tool in uncovering the different kinds of discursive organization of the social world, in this case the discursive construction of adult numeracy classrooms and maths lecture halls and seminar rooms. In neither of these studies, however, was I closely engaged with the numeracy dimension of the research settings. The next study I engaged in involved working with the adult numeracy specialist Betty Johnston, taking a social practice perspective on the numeracy practices of unemployed young people in New South Wales, Australia (Baynham and Johnston 1998; Johnston et al. 1997). What I brought to this research was my experience of researching literacy as social practice, but the study involved extensive collaboration between the adult literacy specialists (myself and Sheilagh Kelly, another UTS colleague) and Betty, so that we developed a methodology that was, I think, equally informed by perspectives from adult literacy and adult numeracy research and thus took us, the research team, on an enormous learning curve into hitherto unfamiliar worlds, in particular what I have termed the number-saturated world.

In an influential paper entitled 'Professional vision', the anthropologist Charles Goodwin describes how various forms of professional training (and I would include research training here) are training in ways of seeing (Goodwin 1994). The archaeologist, geologist or farmer will look at a patch of exposed earth in very different and specialized ways, literally seeing the 'same' patch of earth with different eyes, different again from the vision of the non-specialist. These different ways of seeing are made available though different research paradigms, for example, in critical interpretative research where the emphasis is on reading or deconstructing aspects of the social. Linguistic analysis, for example, enables the analyst to recognize distinctive characteristics of spoken and written language, while sociolinguistics opens up an awareness of the pervasive social variation of language. A grounding in gender theory enables an insight into the role of gender in structuring social relations: we learn to notice the contribution of gender in everyday exchanges. Through working with Betty, I learned to notice the number-saturated world, in the same way that I had earlier learned, in my own research, to notice the ubiquity of literacy events and practices in everyday life, the occurrence of code switching in multilingual conversations or the pervasive gendering of interactions: research training is first and foremost a training in noticing. It is not, of course, enough to notice: the researcher needs to be able to analyse and interpret in order to make what has been noticed work as evidence in advancing a line of enquiry.

In order to make sense of what has been seen we need interpretative tools and frameworks and this I understand as theory. My preferred understanding of theory is, in the neo-Vygotskyan tradition, as a tool for thinking with (compare Wertsch 1985: 77–81): theoretical constructs enable us literally to think thoughts that would not have been possible without them. They enable or open up certain ways of thinking, but typically disable or close down others. Take the much discussed and used construct of 'practice', the focus of papers collected in Baynham and Baker (2002): practice enables us to theorize the intersections between the lived subjectivity of social agents and the structuring social conditions within which agency is produced. In the numeracy practices project we drew on the formulation of practice developed by the Australian sociologist Bob Connell as 'what people do by way of constituting the social relations they live in' (Connell 1987) understanding human action as free action within structural constraints, 'invention within limits' as Bourdieu (1979) memorably puts it. This was my research introduction into the number-saturated world. Before returning to the theme of adult numeracy, I would like to remind you that I have so far introduced two distinct perspectives on research:

1  classroom-based, discourse analytic research using linguistic analysis
2  the analysis of numeracy practices in everyday contexts.

So what about adult numeracy in Australia in the 1990s? Why was adult numeracy not included in the ALLP as I mentioned above? Why not ALLNP? In many ways, adult numeracy was at that time treated implicitly and indeed explicitly in some cases as a subset of adult literacy. This became increasingly a point of contention in the discussions of an increasingly articulate and theoretically informed research and professional adult numeracy community. I can remember the repercussions in my own institution, whose units were typically named as 'language and literacy': it seems that, corresponding to the 'power of numbers' is a power and politics of *naming*. Adult numeracy practitioners and researchers have had to claim a name for themselves that did not involve being subsumed under someone else's nomenclature. At this time, I used to think that adult numeracy, on the analogy of Mike Newman's memorable naming of adult education as the 'poor cousin' (Newman 1979), was in fact the 'poor cousin of a poor cousin', being typically treated as a dependant of the more visible and high-profile adult literacy agenda. I am talking here about the early to mid-1990s and I think the situation has changed dramatically in many ways, in both the UK and Australia, through the actions of adult numeracy practitioners and researchers to exercise their 'agency within limits' and develop a highly visible research agenda. In the context of this relatively weak positioning of adult numeracy, however, it also used to strike me that there was an inbuilt irony at work: in the wider social and policy environment, since numbers were so influential, could so often talk down other forms of evidence and ways of knowing, it seemed highly ironical to me that adult numeracy should be so apparently marginal within the adult basic education context. It is to this issue of the status, power and allure of numbers in the number-saturated world that I would now like to turn, using an example from the numeracy practices data.

In the early stages of the Adult Numeracy Practices Project, the research team decided to keep journals, to record instances in our daily lives where numeracy made an impact, in order to deepen our theoretical understanding of the notion of numeracy practices and their interaction with other structuring categories we had identified such as gender. Here is an example from my journal of the time:

> I go down to BBC Hardware to buy a Father's Day present for my six year old daughter to bring into school for a Father's Day Present Stall that is being organized. My wife has suggested a box of chocolates as a suitable gift, I wanted to get a bottle of wine but the bottle shop was closed. BBC Hardware is open so I go in feeling rather awkward as I am not a DIY person and choose a torch and batteries priced at $5.90 which I think of as a suitable Father's Day present. When I take it to the counter it comes up on the screen at $6.25. I point this out to the man behind the counter and he says I have to take it to another counter where the item can be rung up manually. At the other counter the first man I speak to says: 'It's nothing to do with me, I handle the plumbing sales, I'll get Greg to see to it.' I go to double check the pricing to make sure I'm not wrong. When I get back, Greg is there.
>
> 'This torch is priced at $5.90 but it comes up as $6.25 on the screen,' I repeat.
>
> 'It doesn't worry me,' says Greg and goes on to ring the item up manually.

In my journal, I note that I am left feeling I have made a fuss about something that is basically trivial. I tough it out, however, and the transaction ends amicably. I felt as if my complaint about the pricing was trivial or fussy. Greg seemed to be saying to me: 'Blokes don't worry about a few cents here or there.' Was I being paranoid? It turned out that when we analysed the gendering of numeracy practices in the ethnographic interviews, we identified a 'no worries' attitude to money as a specifically masculine response to daily budgeting. A small exchange around pricing can feed into the analysis of the gendering of numeracy practices, here how fussing about small amounts of money can be construed as unmasculine.

This example illustrated the number saturation of daily life and how it can be understood as part of the identity work of doing masculinity. I would like to finish by illustrating two aspects of number saturation in the professional lives of educational researchers. But first I will contextualize this with a brief illustration of the current pervasiveness of categorization by numbers in the education system. It seems, in educational terms, that we live in a numerically rated world: over recent months, for example, the British papers have published, as they do every year, a number of 'league tables' containing ratings of secondary schools in England, based on numerical data of different sorts: GCSE grades, percentage of days absence etc. All these numerical ratings and rankings are collated into one rank ordering based on performance, a central plank in governmental policy on accountability of schools to performance indicators and published in the newspapers to avid interest which, if I am honest, I must admit I share, while being highly aware of its absurdity. If the school my children attend goes up in the rankings I am pleased, despite all the rational arguments that point out to me the triviality and limitations of many of the measures, if the school drops in the rankings, I might feel concerned. What interests me here is why, against my better judgement, against all commonsense, I am drawn into the numerical ranking, I take pleasure in it, just as I felt a strange pleasure in my school number all those years ago, a number that seemed to give me a new identity.

The issue I am raising here is that of pleasure (and indeed pain), affect or interest in the number-saturated world, which seems to me another dimension of research on the power of numbers, one we associate most closely with the work of Valerie Walkerdine in her landmark work, *The Mastery of Reason* (Walkerdine 1988), but also with Betty Johnston's use of memory work (Johnston 2002, 2003) to explore the subjectivity of mathematical knowledge construction. It seems to me an urgent research agenda to understand more, not just about the social structuring of our mathematized number-saturated world, but also about the pleasure and investment that binds us into the game, simultaneously making us either victors of or victim to it.

I will conclude with two examples of number saturation in the professional lives of educational researchers. My first concerns current changes to the RAE. As is well known, British university departments are, at the time of writing, moving from a system in which they are ranked from 1 to 5* to one in which the work of individual researchers will be ranked from 0 to 4*. So all around the UK, academics as individuals and departments are working to re-invest themselves, in the sense I have just introduced, in a new numerical ranking system: what does it mean to claim your work or that of a colleague as a 1*, 2*, 3* or 4* researcher? How does it feel to be a 0? What are the implications in terms of economic reward and prestige? Huge amounts of resource are being and will be mobilized around these questions over the next few years. Rational voices may point to the limitations, the absurdities even of such measures, to the pressure on academics to overproduce, on quantity as opposed to quality, yet given the existence of such a structuring of research activity, who would want to be outside of it? And to the extent we want to be in it not out of it, we bind ourselves into it, invest in it, take pleasure in it or experience pain as a result of it in ways that it does not take a Foucault to make apparent, although Foucault has, of course, provided us with a theoretical framework within which to think about it. The power of numbers to structure the social world seems to me to be eminently a topic for research, but so are the ways we are as subjects bound into and invested in the resultant structures.

My second example concerns current developments in the evidence-based practice literature to establish hierarchies of evidence for educational research based on the medical model, with RCT (randomized controlled trials) sitting as a 'gold standard' at the top of a hierarchy of evidence (compare Comings 2003). This is another instance of the power of numbers in educational research, which I do not have time in this short chapter to develop. I am certainly not deploring the current resurgence of quantitative methodologies in educational research, which is in many ways to be welcomed, but, as I suggest below, this needs to be contextualized in a broadly multi-method environment, where different methodologies can combine to illuminate urgent educational problems. I also do not want to leave the impression that in this chapter I only want to emphasize the power of numbers to position us as subjects, emphasizing a kind of helpless subjection in the number-saturated world. It is also important to recognize the enabling power of numbers, what one might call the power and possibility of numbers. One way of thinking of numbers is as a semiotic resource, another kind of tool for thinking with. The semiotic resource of numbers and indeed visual representations of numbers, in the shape of graphs and tables for example, interact in multimodal texts, as Jay Lemke points out

(Lemke 1998). The semiotics of number interact with natural language semiotics and visual semiotics in the creation of meaning in such texts.

Let me conclude with an example of the combination of words and numbers in literacy research. In Eve Gregory's and Ann Williams' ethnographic monograph, *City Literacies*, they describe typically recurring literacy events in which older siblings in the Bangladeshi families they visited interacted with younger siblings supporting their reading with a range of strategies (Gregory and Williams 2000; Chapter 6). Where do these strategies come from? Gregory and Williams quantify the strategies used by the older children and compare them with those used by their reading teachers. The quantification is represented in a series of bar graphs, which provide an elegant and convincing visual representation of the similarities between the reading support strategies of older children and teachers. Quantification is used in a qualitative, thickly described, ethnographic study to establish a convincing relationship. The power and economy of numbers and graphs to identify and portray relationships, establishing relational meanings, interacts with the texture of the ethnographic account in a productive way. Other kinds of data evident in the same chapter include photographs of children interacting with text and transcripts of spoken language data at home and at school. Work such as this provides grounds for optimism about the potential of both numbers and words as interacting ways of knowing, deepening and extending our research repertoire.

## Conclusion

In this chaper, in discussing the emergence of adult numeracy as a distinctive field of activity, I have suggested that accompanying the power and politics of numbers there is a power and politics of naming. I have briefly identified three research methodologies which I see as complementary from my own repertoire:

- linguistic analysis of the discursive construction of classrooms
- researching social practices in a range of domains and settings
- researching the subjectivities and processes of subject production which bind us into social practices such as numerical categorization and grading.

It is through such continued multi-method critical research activity that we can develop the arguments to have with ourselves and with policy in order to move our research agenda and other social agenda forward in more rational ways. I have emphasized the ways we are typically positioned in the number-saturated world, yet finish by recalling, as Connell and indeed Foucault in their different ways suggest, that power opens up possibilities: that an alternative title for this chapter might have been 'The Power and Possibilities of Numbers'.

## References

Baynham, M. (1995) 'Reading as situated social practice: what counts as a proper reading in an adult numeracy classroom?' *Prospect*, 10(2): 18–26.

Baynham, M. (1996) 'Humour as an interpersonal resource in adult numeracy classrooms'. *Language and Education*, 10: 2–3.

Baynham, M. and Baker, D. (2002) 'Literacy and numeracy practices'. Special Issue of *Ways of Knowing Journal*, 2(1).

Baynham, M. and Johnston B. (1998) ' "Invention within limits": numeracy practices of young unemployed people'. *Literacy & Numeracy Studies*, 8(1): 51–65.

Baynham, M., Wood, L. and Smith, G. (1995) 'Communication needs of mathematicians' in Hunting, R.P., Fitzsimons, G., Clarkson, P. and Bishop, A.J. (eds) *Regional Collaboration in Mathematics Education, Proceedings of ICMI Regional Conference*. Monash University: Melbourne, pp. 775–84.

Bourdieu, P. (1979) *Outline of a Theory of Practice*. Cambridge: Cambridge University Press.

Comings, J. (2003) 'Evidence-based adult education: a perspective from the United States'. Paper given at National Research and Development Centre for Adult Literacy and Numeracy Conference 'What counts as evidence for what purposes in research in Adult Literacy, Numeracy and ESOL?'

Connell, B. ( 1987) *Gender and Power: Society, the Person and Sexual Politics*. Cambridge: Polity Press.

Goodwin, C. (1994) 'Professional vision'. *American Anthropologist*, 96(3): 606–33.

Gregory, E. and Williams, A. (2000) *City Literacies: Learning to Read Across Generations and Cultures*. London: Routledge.

Johnston, B. (2002) 'Capturing numeracy practices: memory work and time'. *Ways of Knowing Journal*, 2(1): 33–44.

Johnston, B. (2003) 'A view from somewhere: identity and collective memory work'. Paper given at National Research and Development Centre for Adult Literacy and Numeracy Conference, 'What counts as evidence for what purposes in research in Adult Literacy, Numeracy and ESOL?'

Johnston, B., Baynham, M., Kelly, S., Barlow, K. and Marks, G. (1997) *Numeracy in Practice: Effective Pedagogy in Numeracy for Unemployed Young People*. Sydney: Australian National Training Authority, Department of Employment Education, Training and Youth Affairs.

Lemke, J. (1998) 'Multiplying meaning: visual and verbal semiotics in scientific text' in Martin, J.R. and Veel, R. (eds) *Reading Science*. London: Routledge.

Newman, M. (1979) *The Poor Cousin: A Study of Adult Education*. London, Boston, MA: Allen & Unwin.

Walkerdine, V. (1988) *The Mastery of Reason*. London: Routledge.

Wertsch, J. (1985) *Vygotsky and the Social Formation of Mind*. Cambridge, MA: Harvard University Press.

# 9 Social–Cultural Approach to Adult Numeracy: Issues for Policy and Practice

*Diana Coben*

## Introduction

With the publication of the report of Professor Adrian Smith's inquiry into post-14 mathematics education in February 2004 (Smith 2004), adult numeracy education is at last moving from the margins to the mainstream of educational policy. From invisibility in the 1970s and 1980s, subsumed within adult literacy, adult numeracy emerged as an 'adult basic skill' in the 1990s, culminating in the publication of the *Moser Report* (DfEE 1999) and the inception of the government's Skills for Life (DfEE 2001) strategy to improve adult literacy and numeracy in England; but adult numeracy still lagged behind adult literacy in policy and practice. Now it features in the first major government report on mathematics education since the *Cockcroft Report* (DES/WO 1982).

Current structures, qualifications and development in 'adult basic numeracy' are outlined in Sections 3.49–3.53 of the *Smith Report* (Smith 2004: 69–71). Concerns about adult numeracy education are outlined as follows:

*Concerns with adult numeracy*

**4.40** There is some concern that employers are not yet fully recognizing the new Adult Numeracy qualifications. It has also been impressed on the Inquiry that adults want to learn mathematics for a variety of reasons, often not concerned with gaining qualifications. Respondents to the Inquiry have expressed some concern that, at present, test questions tend to reflect traditional 'school mathematics', in the sense of testing mathematical procedures posed as contextualized problems with multiple choice answers. It is felt that these tests do not necessarily fit well with the idea of individual adult learner plans and properly exploit adult learners' contexts. It is also felt that the present tests at levels 1 and 2 disadvantage ESOL learners and those with dyslexia or dyscalculia, or low levels of literacy. Many respondents feel that:

- numeracy capabilities have generally been undervalued, under-developed and under-resourced;
- support and learning programmes have been few in number and poor in quality;
- materials and qualifications have been child rather than adult centred;
- teachers have been inadequately trained and in many cases specialist numeracy teachers have been replaced by literacy teachers, often working beyond their own levels of mathematical competence;
- performance and alignment with GSCE Mathematics and National Curriculum levels is highlighting inadequacies in the appropriateness of these programmes to prepare young people for adult life in general and the workplace in particular.

**4.41** Respondents to the Inquiry are clear that the adult numeracy strategy is a challenging and demanding one for teachers and learners alike. Progress could easily be undermined by:

- uncertainties surrounding the teaching and assessment of mathematics in general and in particular the future of GCSE Mathematics and key skills;
- the limited pool of competent and confident teachers of mathematics and numeracy;
- the lack of employer engagement in raising the skill base of new employees.

In Chapter 6, we suggest that the national infrastructure for the support of the teaching of mathematics include specific support for teachers of adult numeracy. (Smith 2004: 95–6)

Many of the *Smith Report* recommendations cross education sectors, while some refer specifically to adult numeracy; these are paraphrased here:

*Recommendation 4.7* recommends an immediate review of current problems of delivery, content, assessment and availability of courses at levels 1–3, including adult numeracy, in order to identify scope for improvements in and potential rationalization of this provision, including opportunities for more systematic integration of ICT in teaching and learning, as part of the longer term design of a new 14–19 pathway structure for mathematics (see Recommendation 4.11).

*Recommendation 4.11* recommends that funding be provided for up to three curriculum and assessment development studies of variants of pathway models and approaches, including trialling, feedback and modification and an assessment of the workload implications. The aim of this exercise will be to inform the selection of a preferred pathway model to form part of the reformed 14–19 structure in England and possible parallel developments in Wales and Northern Ireland.

*Recommendation 6.10* The national infrastructure for the support of the teaching and learning of mathematics should set up formal collaborative links with the National Research and Development Centre for Adult Literacy and Numeracy (NRDC), with a view to exploring how best to support teachers of adult numeracy.

The *Smith Report* includes possible models of provision, including one where mathematics en (entry level) is followed by 'numerical literacy' at level 1, moving on to 'quantitative literacy' at level 2 (see Smith 2004: 100, Figure 4.2). In the model simultaneously developed by the Tomlinson Working Group on 14–19 Reform (Tomlinson 2004), the term 'functional mathematics' appears, with reference to 'end-users' and preparation for 'adult life – this should include financial literacy alongside the application of mathematics in a variety of other real world contexts'.

Work is underway on implementing the *Smith Report* recommendations and, more generally, carrying forward research and development in this area. In England, the Qualifications and Curriculum Authority (QCA) has been asked to undertake work on several curriculum and qualifications projects, including the development of mathematics pathways.[1] Also in England, Maths4Life,[2] a three-year project funded

---

[1] I am working on one of these pathways projects, the Developing Curriculum Pathways in Mathematics project, a collaboration between King's College London and the Awarding Body, EdExcel. This project began in Spring 2005 and ends in 2006.

[2] Maths4Life is being developed by a consortium of partners led by the NRDC with the Language and Literacy Unit Plus (LLU+) at London South Bank University as its main partner; I am a member of the Maths4Life Strategic Management Team (www.maths4life.org/).

by the DfES Skills for Life Strategy Unit, aims to stimulate a positive approach to teaching and learning in adult numeracy and mathematics, combining research and practice to produce teaching and learning resources and guidance. In Scotland, where a model of adult literacies[3] education is in place, the Scottish Executive has published a report on adult numeracy education, *Adult Numeracy: Shifting the Focus* (Coben 2005), which makes recommendations intended to bring adult numeracy more sharply into focus within adult literacies policy and provision.

As adult numeracy begins to take its place in the landscape of educational policy in the UK, it may be time to move from a critical (for example, Coben 2001; Coben and Chanda 2000) to a critically creative phase in policy analysis. In that spirit, I want to consider how a socio-cultural approach to adult numeracy might inform educational policy in this area.

## Socio-cultural approaches to adult numeracy and mathematics education

There is considerable debate within the adult numeracy and mathematics education community about what may loosely be called socio-cultural approaches, often contrasted with constructivist approaches (Cobb 1994), although the boundaries between these positions are somewhat permeable. Constructivist epistemologies of mathematics education view mathematics learning as a process, whereby knowledge of mathematics is gained by doing mathematics, rather than a product. Constructivist educators tend either to focus on ways in which the individual learner makes sense of mathematics (after Piaget) or, increasingly, see learning as an activity in which shared mathematical meanings are constructed socially (after Vygotsky) (Dossey 1992; Sierpinska and Lerman 1996). Barbara Jaworski has pointed out that debates between 'radical and 'social' constructivists discussed by Paul Ernest (Ernest 1994) parallel debates between protagonists of these two positions (Jaworski 1994).

Socio-cultural epistemologies of mathematics education (Atweh, Forgasz and Nebres 2001) are making headway in the adult mathematics education research domain, rooted as they are in respect for adults'

---

[3] The new Adult Literacy and Numeracy Curriculum Framework for Scotland (2005) is available on the Communities Scotland website (www.communitiesscotland.gov.uk). See the discussion below on socio-cultural approaches for more on a pluralistic concept of 'literacies'.

'commonsense' knowledge in their everyday lives. For example, the work of Jean Lave (Lave 1988; Lave and Wenger 1991), in theorizing situated cognition has been influential, together with studies of informal mathematics practices in Brazil (Carraher 1991) and elsewhere. Jeff Evans' work on adults' numerate practices also stems from a socio-cultural constructivist perspective (Evans 2000), as does much research on ethnomathematics, the mathematics of cultural groups (D'Ambrosio 1997; Powell and Frankenstein 1997).

What these approaches have in common is a deep regard for the social context in which people's actions, including their mathematical actions and interpretations of information involving mathematics, have meaning. They are based in a view of the human being as a social being and of mathematics as human activity.

## How might a socio-cultural approach to numeracy inform policy?

In the remaining part of this chapter, I want to draw on my discussion in the NRDC review of research in adult numeracy (Coben 2003) to explore what light might be shed on policy issues in adult numeracy by viewing them through the lens of the new literacy studies. For the purposes of this discussion I shall focus on the following characteristics of the new literacy studies: a pluralistic conception of literacy (that is, literacies); and a distinction between 'autonomous' and 'ideological' models of literacy. So the question becomes: How might a pluralistic conception of numeracy, expressed in terms of a distinction between 'autonomous' and 'ideological' models, inform policy in adult numeracy education?

## A pluralistic conception: numeracy within literacies or 'numeracies'?

In the new literacy studies, language and literacy (and, although this is not always specified: numeracy) are seen as social practices rather than technical skills to be learned in formal education (Street 2001). Since there is a multiplicity of these social practices, it is argued that there is also a multiplicity of literacies. This view has been challenged by Kress (2000), who argues that this is to atomize literacy, an argument that applies with equal force to numeracy conceived as an element within literacies, or to a pluralized concept of numeracy: 'numeracies'.

Ironically, one of the problems with the model of numeracy embodied in the Skills for Life adult numeracy core curriculum (ANCC)

(BSA 2001) is precisely that it is atomized, although in terms of mathematics rather than social practice, with separate mathematical elements ticked off in the process of education. In the ANCC, social practices are relegated to examples of ways in which the learner's context might relate to a particular element. The idea is that the curriculum is context free, learners bring their contexts to the learning environment and the teacher's task is to bring the two together in effective teaching geared to the adult numeracy standards (QCA 2000) negotiated with the learner and set out in an individual learning plan. Learners' individual and social practices (conceived as their 'contexts') are incorporated into a hierarchically organized, skills-based curriculum. The discourse of human resource development, with its associated managerialism and technicism (Gee, Hull and Lankshear 1996), predominates.

A pluralistic conception of numeracies as situated social practice might produce a different kind of curriculum, with the learner's situated practices as the starting point. But learners' practices and contexts differ: one person's familiar context is another person's alien territory and issues around the relationship between context and mathematics and the possibility of 'transfer' of mathematics between contexts are complex (Evans 2000). Somehow, the mathematics to be learned must be identified and learned. Indeed, in my experience as an adult numeracy teacher the issue of 'seeing through to the maths' in a situation is crucial: once people see that there is something mathematical to be done which produces a way through a problem, they may find the actual mathematics relatively straightforward. Sometimes they recognize a mathematical operation they have done before, sometimes they work the problem out from scratch, on their own or with help from the teacher or fellow students. These 'Eureka moments' are one of the things that make adult numeracy teaching worthwhile.

This is not to say that mathematics does not need to be taught to adults. Indeed, this is a potential weakness in a social practices conception of numeracy, that it could be seen as implying that adults' practices are so rich in mathematical knowledge and understanding that no teaching – or even further learning – is necessary. This is an educational cul de sac, and it points up a significant difference between numeracy and literacy: the fact that reading and writing a language one already speaks is not analogous to 'doing mathematics' or 'being numerate', because most people do not 'speak mathematics as a first language': they need to be taught it.

## 'Autonomous' and 'ideological' models of numeracy?

In the 'autonomous' model literacy is seen as having consequences in and of itself, irrespective of context. By contrast, in the 'ideological' model,

> [L]iteracy not only varies with social context and with cultural norms and discourses regarding, for instance, identity, gender and belief, but ... its uses and meanings are always embedded in relations of power. It is in this sense that literacy is always 'ideological' – it always involves contests over meanings, definitions and boundaries and struggles for control of the literacy agenda. (Street 2001: 18)

In the NRDC review of research in adult numeracy I asked whether Street's distinction works for numeracy and decided that it works up to a point, depending on which concept of numeracy is being used (Coben et al. 2003: 29). I note that although a view of numeracy as culturally determined and socially formed practice(s) is common in the main-stream research and critical literature on adult numeracy and mathematics, this is not usually framed in terms of the new literacy studies. Computational concepts of numeracy (Glenn 1978) may certainly be seen as 'autonomous' in Street's sense. Similarly, concepts of numeracy that view it as social practice, varying according to context, may be seen as 'ideological' in Street's sense. However, the distinction has not been widely applied to numeracy, which is perhaps surprising since there are close links between literacy and numeracy practice in the UK and Australia, two countries where the new literacy studies have made an impact.

## A new numeracy studies?

I also noted that there are exceptions: studies in numeracy which build on conceptions of literacies developed in the new literacy studies, hinting at the possible emergence of a new numeracy studies. For example, Betty Johnston discusses 'numeracies' (Johnston 1999) and Dave Baker has argued that the Adult Literacy and Basic Skills Unit (ALBSU, now the Basic Skills Agency, BSA), has promulgated an autonomous model of numeracy as culture and value free and that this is the dominant model. He argues that the existence of multiple numeracies must lead to the questioning of standards based on this model (Baker 1998). Also, work on schooled and community numeracies by a team of researchers (including Alison Tomlin, working with Baker and Street) had as one of its dimensions the consideration of how far a social literacies approach could be applied in the field of mathematics education (Baker, Street and Tomlinson 2000). Tomlin casts doubt on how far this may be possible, given the invisibility of many 'numeracy events' and practices (Tomlin 2002). For example, mathematics may be 'done in the head' and hence invisible to the observer, or it may be deeply embedded in activities which the person concerned does not regard as mathematical. This last point raises a key methodological consideration: should researchers – or teachers – avoid imputing mathematical thinking and other activity to individuals in situations where those individuals deny that mathematics is involved?

Ethnomathematics has affinities with Street's approach, as might be expected, given their common roots in anthropology. Nevertheless, proponents of a social practices approach to adult numeracy do not couch their research in terms of the new literacy studies and debates within ethnomathematics have gone on in a different part of the forest.

The absence of more widespread use or discussion of these approaches in relation to adult numeracy may simply reflect the relatively under-theorized state of adult numeracy by comparison with adult literacy. Alternatively, it could be argued that a view of numeracy as culturally determined and socially formed practice(s) is implicit – and sometimes explicit – in the mainstream research and critical literature on adult numeracy, but that, as already noted, this view is not usually framed in terms of the new literacy studies. It should also be remembered that Street's distinction between autonomous and ideological literacy was made in reaction against the claim that literacy is the hallmark of culture, a claim that is rarely made for numeracy, especially since it fell from the lofty position accorded it when the term was first used in the *Crowther Report* (DES 1959) to denote familiarity with the scientific and numerate disciplines, so that the need to counter such a view hardly exists.

Numeracy is also sometimes casually included in 'literacies' with scant regard to its particularities, so that it becomes as invisible within literacies as it has been when subsumed within literacy.

## Conclusion

So where does this leave us? What does a socio-cultural approach have to offer to policy studies in adult numeracy education? Would a socio-cultural approach relieve us of the obsession with skills at the expense of knowledge and understanding, the paraphernalia of learner targets, a segmented curriculum with its roots in primary education, and concerns about accountability and standards that are such a strong feature of the current public policy scene? Perhaps. It remains to be seen whether numeracy will fare better in policy terms as part of a broader vision of mathematics education than it has done when yoked to literacy. It will be interesting to see how numeracy fares as part of literacies in the new Scottish curriculum. In England it should be remembered that the Smith and Tomlinson agendas, while broader, do not necessarily preclude numeracy continuing to be treated as a 'basic skill'. Much will depend on the nature of the pathways for progression which are developed and approved and on the meaning given within them to terms such as 'functional mathematics'.

Adult numeracy and mathematics are currently on policymakers' agendas as they have not been hitherto. How should numeracy educators – practitioners and researchers – respond? The Australian experience may be instructive here. A press release accompanying the publication of a report by the Australian Council for Adult Literacy (ACAL 2001) said: 'Ten years ago Australia was at the forefront of adult literacy and numeracy teaching, learning and research. Now, we do not even have a national policy and we are going backwards.' Mahatma Gandhi once described policy as 'a temporary creed liable to be changed, but while it holds good it has got to be pursued with apostolic zeal.' If true, it is especially important to make the most of the opportunity offered by Skills for Life and the Smith and Tomlinson reports, and, in Scotland, the new curriculum framework, to contribute to the creation of insights and educational practices that stand the test of time. That must include taking adult numeracy education seriously on its own terms, with an equal, rather than a subservient relationship to literacy and language studies. It must also involve seeking to recognize both the mathematical aspects of adults' social and individual practices and the power of mathematics as the discipline on which numeracy is built.

# References

ACAL (2001) 'News release – parties must address Australia's poor literacy and numeracy levels, www.acal.edu.au/publications/papers/news/ElecnNewsRe16ct01.html (accessed 2 July 2005).

Atweh, B., Forgasz, H. and Nebres, B. (eds) (2001) *Sociocultural Research on Mathematics Education: An International Perspective.* Mahwah, NJ: Laurence Erlbaum Associates Inc.

Baker, D. (1998) 'Numeracy as social practice'. *Literacy and Numeracy Studies*, 8(1): 37–51.

Baker, D.A., Street, B.V. and Tomlin, A. (2000) 'Schooled and community numeracies: understanding social factors and "under achievement" in numeracy' in Matos, J.F. and Santos, M. (eds) *Mathematics Education and Society*. Proceedings of the Second International Mathematics Education and Society Conference (MES2), 26–31 March, 2000. Lisbon, Portugal: Centro de Investigação em Educação da Faculdade de Ciências, Universidade de Lisboa: 158–68.

BSA (2001) *Adult Numeracy Core Curriculum*. London: Cambridge Training and Development on behalf of the Basic Skills Agency.

Carraher, D. (1991) 'Mathematics learned in and out of school: a selective review of studies from Brazil' in Harris, M. (ed.) *Schools, Mathematics and Work*. London: Falmer Press.

Cobb, P. (1994) 'Where is the mind? Constructivist and sociocultural perspectives on mathematical development'. *Educational Researcher*, 23(7): 13–20.

Coben, D. (2001) 'Fact, fiction and moral panic: the changing adult numeracy curriculum in England', in FitzSimons, G.E., O'Donoghue, J. and Coben, D. (eds) *Adult and Life-long Education in Mathematics: Papers from Working Group for Action 6, 9th International Congress on Mathematical Education, ICME 9*. Melbourne: Language Australia in association with Adults Learning Mathematics – A Research Forum (ALM): 125–53.

Coben, D. (2005) *Adult Numeracy: Shifting the Focus. A Report and Recommendations on Adult Numeracy in Scotland*. Edinburgh: Learning Connections, Scottish Executive.

Coben, D. and Chanda, N. (2000) 'Teaching "not less than maths, but more": an overview of recent developments in adult numeracy teacher development in England – with a sidelong glance at Australia' in Coben, D., O'Donoghue, J. and FitzSimons, G.E. (eds) *Perspectives on Adults Learning Mathematics: Research and Practice*. Dordrecht, The Netherlands: Kluwer Academic Publishers.

Coben, D., Colwell, D., Macrae, S., Boales, J. Brown, M. and Rhodes, V. (2003) *Adult Numeracy: Review of Research and Related Literature*. London: National Research and Development Centre for Adult Literacy and Numeracy (NRDC).

D'Ambrosio, U. (1997) 'Ethnomathematics and its place in the history and pedagogy of mathematics' in Powell, A.B. and Frankenstein, M. (eds) *Ethnomathematics: Challenging Eurocentrism in Mathematics Education*. Albany, NY: State University of New York Press.

DES (1959) *15 to 18, A Report of the Central Advisory Committee for Education* (England). London: Department of Education and Science (DES).

DES/WO (1982) *Mathematics Counts: Report of the Committee of Inquiry into the Teaching of Mathematics in Schools*. London: Department of Education and Science/Welsh Office.

DfEE (1999) *A Fresh Start: Improving Literacy and Numeracy. The Report of the Working Group Chaired by Sir Claus Moser*. London: Department for Education and Employment.

DfEE (2001) *Skills for Life: The National Strategy for Improving Adult Literacy and Numeracy Skills*. London: Department for Education and Employment (UK).

Dossey, J.A. (1992) 'The nature of mathematics: its role and its influence' in Grouws, D. *Handbook of Research on Mathematics Teaching and Learning*. New York: Macmillan.

Ernest, P. (ed.) (1994) *Mathematics Education and Philosophy: An International Perspective*. Studies in Mathematics Education Series, No. 3. London: Falmer Press.

Evans, J. (2000) *Adults' Mathematical Thinking and Emotions: A Study of Numerate Practices*. London: RoutledgeFalmer, Taylor & Francis Group.

Gee, J., Hull, C. and Lankshear, C. (1996) *The New Work Order: Behind the Language of the New Capitalism*. Sydney and Boulder, CA: Allen & Unwin and Westview Press.

Glenn, J.A. (ed.) (1978) *The Third R: Towards a Numerate Society*. London: Harper & Row.

Jaworski, B. (1994) *Investigating Mathematics Teaching: A Constructivist Enquiry*. Bristol, PA: Falmer Press.

Johnston, B. (1999) 'Adult numeracy' in Wagner, D.A., Venezky, R. and Street, B.V. (eds) *Literacy: An International Handbook*. Boulder, CO: Westview Press.

Kress, G. (2000) 'The futures of literacy'. *RaPAL Bulletin*: 42.

Lave, J. (1988) *Cognition in Practice: Mind, Mathematics and Culture in Everyday Life*. Cambridge: Cambridge University Press.

Lave, J. and Wenger E. (1991) *Situated Learning: Legitimate Peripheral Participation*. Cambridge: Cambridge University Press.

Powell, A.B. and Frankenstein, M. (eds) (1997) *Ethnomathematics: Challenging Eurocentrism in Mathematics Education*. Albany, NY: State University of New York Press.

QCA (2000) *National Standards for Adult Literacy and Numeracy*. London: Qualifications and Curriculum Authority.

Sierpinska, A. and Lerman, S. (1996) 'Epistemologies of mathematics and of mathematics education' in Bishop, A.J., Clements, K., Keitel, C., Kilpatrick, J. and Laborde, C. *International Handbook of Mathematics Education*. Dordrecht, The Netherlands: Kluwer Academic Publishers.

Smith, A. (2004) *Making Mathematics Count: The Report of Professor Adrian Smith's Inquiry into Post-14 Mathematics Education*. London: The Stationery Office.

Street, B.V. (2001) 'Contexts for literacy work: the "new orders" and the "new literacy studies"' in Crowther, J., Hamilton, M. and Tett, L. (eds) *Powerful Literacies*. Leicester, NIACE.

Tomlin, A. (2002) '"Real life" in everyday and academic maths' in Johansen, L.Ø. and Wedege, T. (eds) *Numeracy for Empowerment and Democracy? Proceedings of the 8th International Conference of Adults Learning Mathematics – A Research Forum (ALM8)*. Roskilde, Denmark: Centre for Research in Learning Mathematics, Roskilde University, in association with Adults Learning Mathematics – A Research Forum: 156–64.

Tomlinson, M. (2004) *14–19 Curriculum and Qualifications Reform. Final Report of the Working Group on 14–19 Reform*. Annesley: Department for Education and Skills.

# 10 Measuring Up: Practitioners Researching Numeracy

*Mark Baxter, Eamonn Leddy, Liz Richards, Alison Tomlin and Topo Wresniwiro*

## Introduction

This chapter is by the four teacher–researchers and the researcher who worked together on a 20-month (2002–2004) teacher–research project, *Teaching and Learning Common Measures, especially at Entry level.*[1] We focus on our experiences of the project rather than the project's findings, which are available in our report (Baxter et al. forthcoming). The teachers worked in three colleges of further education and two prisons; we taught generic numeracy courses, rather than, for example, numeracy embedded in vocational courses, or family numeracy. We had paid release from work for a day a week (sometimes made up of two hours here and half a day there). This chapter makes the links between research, policy and practice highlighted throughout this book through a commitment to practitioner involvement in research and the activities and insights generated from this.

One of the team wrote in his research diary that being made up differently, brought up in different environments and accustomed to different surroundings and opportunities makes us (everyone) what we are. What we shared was our work in adult numeracy education, but our length of experience of teaching mathematics covered a spread from a few years to the whole of a (now middle-aged) working life; and our own knowledge, use and enjoyment of mathematics in various contexts, including in education and other jobs, varied as much as students'. One had hated maths vehemently at school and it only clicked when he could see its practical purpose. In contrast, another, herself well-qualified in mathematics and working as a numeracy coordinator, wanted to stretch her aching grey cells. The NRDC's practitioner research programme included the opportunity to take a

---

[1] The project was funded by the National Research and Development Centre for adult literacy and numeracy (www.nrdc.org.uk) and directed by Diana Coben and Margaret Brown, King's College London.

master's research methods module, that is, gain public recognition of research skills which might contribute to career development, but only one of us took that up. Most embarked on the project only with a view to learning more for ourselves, contributing to research, and improving the ways in which we teach numeracy, or at least measures, but through the project we came to see measures as central to mathematics itself.

Measurement should be ideal for using both discussion and practical exercises through bringing in a huge range of students' individual backgrounds and current experiences and exposing that there are many ways to get to an acceptable solution to a given problem, encompassing problem-solving techniques, a variety of cultural approaches and discussion points such as approximation, estimation and accuracy. Our approach to measurement – and by extension, to other aspects of numeracy as well – is consistent with a social practices account in that we recognize and value cultural diversity and multiplicity in the sorts of mathematics that people use and the ways they deal with mathematical problems.

Measurement is part of the adult numeracy core curriculum (DfES & Basic Skills Agency 2001) and we apparently taught it, but as the project developed, we raised questions about whether we were really teaching it at all. In craft and science courses, measurement is taught, and examined, quite differently. Were we looking at teaching measurement as defined by the core curriculum, or practical applied measurement? It always seemed to be underdeveloped in the classroom, the logistical difficulties of doing practical measuring, weighing and capacity activities, often having to provide our own equipment, usually meant it was visited minimally. There is not much measure in numeracy examinations, and it is of an abstract nature (our website (www.nrdc. org.uk/measures) includes examples of particularly poor examination questions). Classroom work sometimes ended up being dominated by converting between units.

Of all the topics we teach it was the one that many students found hardest, even though the concepts, for us, seemed simple. We believed that if we had taught it well, the students would have found it easy and practically useful; they didn't.

## Doing research

We sorted out ideas in team meetings. They were compelling and enlightening, in one memory; in another, they were taken up with gripes about how our teaching and the students' learning or enjoyment was being stifled by management and government initiatives. It felt more rewarding than a staffroom moan because there was a feeling at that time that there was a slight chance it could change something.

Every meeting was a chance to talk about education in broad terms. We got fresh ideas from those teaching in different environments. The records of our meetings formed a substantial part of our data, but until late in the day it was not clear how we would ever develop a coherent story.

At the meetings we discussed the detailed notes from our classes, in which we reflected on our teaching. Whizz, whizz, whizz ... we soon became swamped with 'data' and found it too time consuming to create, read and comment on it all. Although we had an apparently tightly defined set of research questions, almost everything about our work turned out to be relevant. We realized we could include everything and anything, and while that might be liberating, sometimes we felt we had too little focus.

There were particular issues for teachers in prisons. Drug dealers had a working knowledge of the measurement of weight and were familiar with equivalent fractions as long as they were 1/4s, 1/8s and 1/16s. We were constantly on the lookout for practical contexts for measuring, and here it was – but aside from the ethics, why teach people what they know already? Education is to take you somewhere new.

Keeping a reflective log was very hard. We tried making notes during the classes, but that took time from the students. There was no break between classes in which to write notes, and tape recorders could not pick up exchanges between students (and we could not tape in the prisons). Student interviews were not always successful either – the researcher used her first interview as a good example of bad interviewing. Just meeting students was hard enough. Student A cannot do this week. Next week? OK! Oops, the teacher's daughter is sick and he misses the session. Next week again? OK! Oh, no, the student's son is sick. The week after that, we must do assessments ...

We could not collect all the relevant data, but we were concerned that what we, as individuals, recorded because it was significant to us might not be significant to others (teachers, researchers or students) – and that what we overlooked as insignificant may later have turned out to be significant.

So it was hard to collect data because there was too much of it – but at times there was none. In one prison there was a lot of pressure for the men to pass examinations. Work on measures was not very relevant, and the teacher felt awkward and unable to contribute to the research project. Few prisoners were brought to the education centre (for reasons beyond the control of education staff); the teacher had to go out on the wings to find the students, with a lot of recruiting done by word of mouth.

In the further education colleges the students were grouped into classes organized into levels, but the teachers worked with a wide range of courses of which only a few were at entry level. Some of those courses worked across a wide range of mathematics, because the students had been assessed on the basis of their literacy or language, rather than numeracy, skills.

Meanwhile we felt under the pressure of having to come up with deep and meaningful results to help the nation.

Throughout the process of collecting data we debated the meaning of measures and how to make them more meaningful in the classroom. As we came to see measures as a root of, and route to, mathematics, we started to use measurement more widely across the numeracy curriculum to actively illustrate a range of processes. We already used time and money, measures that are familiar to the point of dominating our lives, as contexts for work on the four rules, but we realized there was no reason why length, weight and capacity could not also be used to practise number skills and problem solving. We have put those ideas into a collection of teaching and learning resources, including a scheme of work organized around measures and classroom activities (www.nrdc.org.uk/measures). Some of us tried the new activities in our own classes, but some of the ideas were not tried out until we and some students organized an open workshop a few weeks before the project finished. At the workshop we found it very difficult, even with the full research team there, to observe students and assist them at the same time. With hindsight we can see we should have developed materials sooner; we then all could have tried them in different classes and compared how we felt they went.

## Teaching, professional development and time

As experienced tutors we felt that we had been subject, year on year, to more demands on our time – more teaching hours per week, more administration tasks, more evidence to be collected to justify the expenditure of public money ... We had less time and energy to reflect on our practice and also, significantly, less local professional development time: it was usurped by management for training staff in 'required' and ever-changing systems to record retention, monitor progress and achievement and so on.

The project gave us a buzz in the head about our teaching – an opportunity to question ourselves about our own learning and teaching. As teachers we are always trying new things out, trying to find the perfect lesson, to find the right answer to the problem, and having to edit our teaching notes for others to read made us much more reflective.

The project gave us the space and the peace of mind to try things out; change encourages reflection and reflection encourages change. We learned from each other as well as from students.

But such projects do depend on time. One of us has conducted more recently a small project in the context of prison education, but has been refused the paid release to enable him to undertake a more substantial study. Another changed jobs during the *Measures* project, and so had no released time. He hoped to continue in his own time with the project, but his workload (which takes up teachers' 'own time' as well as work time) made it impossible. Later he was offered an opportunity to join a teacher research project (that is, the college would be paid for his time), but management refused to release him.

## Relationships with research and researchers

A research diary entry before an Adults Learning Mathematics conference: 'I have some kind of doodles in my head what it might look like in the conference. That's all I can do. I leave it at this point.'

Conferences are a focus of life for researchers: write the paper, submit it, present it, see it published ... As we attended more conferences we gained experience in presenting our work, facing an audience and answering questions. We have mixed experiences of how much we learned, and how much other researchers seemed to be willing to learn from practitioners. One of us attended an international conference three weeks after joining the project, and was initially baffled by the technical jargon: methodology, quantitative and qualitative data analysis ... We settled into that language. We learned a great deal from resourceful and critical teachers and researchers. Some of that learning was too gradual to notice, but there were some moments when we noticed our own questions and ideas shifting. One of our reports, from a workshop run jointly with another NRDC teacher research project, includes participants' images of mathematics (Baker et al. 2003); another includes participants' comments on teaching and learning measures for us to address as our project continued (Baxter et al. 2003).

We are, however, critical of the relationship of (some) professional researchers to practitioners' research. At an international conference we were disappointed by the lack of interest from the professional researchers in our workshop 'On being a Teacher/Researcher'.[2] Research-

---

[2] Run jointly with teacher–researchers from another NRDC project, Making Numeracy Teaching Meaningful.

ers in adult numeracy should not be working in a vacuum: surely students and staff would be vital to their work, so the lack of attendance at our workshop was surprising. We started to question the validity of their research.

Research funding seems to ensure that people can fly around from one country to another, to conferences where the delegates and speakers are largely the same as the conference they have just come from. There is an enormous gulf between (a number of) the 'academics' and the practitioners. The researchers feed off the practice. They study it from a range of distances and angles, they digest it, pass ideas around and publish 'papers'. They have their own jargon, and their conversations and discussions are frequently peppered with the names and dates of authors and articles. If they taught, they wouldn't need to do the research to discover something that all practitioners know.

So we have become rather cynical about educational research. Contrariwise, we would not have taken part in the project if we did not value research. We recognize that 'knowing' something may not help arguments about adult numeracy education; research can be used to support a particular case. We, and many of our colleagues we suspect, tend to plod along seemingly without needing to know about all this stuff (we have no background in theories of teaching), yet we might think that research into all aspects of adult numeracy should be at the heart of what we do and how we do it. There seems to be a parallel with many of the students in our project, who exist happily in their lives without the need, as they see it, for an understanding of measurement – yet we, as practitioners, feel that measurement is at the heart of mathematics.

There is another element in the weakness of the links between research and practice: employers. They may want the kudos of having their staff involved in a research project, but ours were not so willing to allow time off at times that helped us meet. Like teachers, they see researchers as remote and not properly engaged with the classroom. When magazines and reports are circulated in the workplace, teachers, timetabled to the hilt, do not have time to read them.

Ideas are imposed on teachers from managers without discussion: this is the way it shall be. We do not, for example, know whether current management tools and government-sponsored materials have been researched. They include particular forms of individual learning plans, learning styles approaches and the Skills for Life materials (DfES n.d.): are they the only answer? How were they trialled? Who has compared them to alternatives? Have we enough evidence about what life was like before them, and therefore what has changed?

When in the thick of it teachers are looking for something concrete to use. After years of being time challenged in our work, we have developed a modus operandi of taking on board anything that is clearly positive, practical, easy to use and more-or-less immediate in its effect. This has left us rather impatient with anything 'fuzzy round the edges', not personally relevant, ineffective or that seems to be just wishful thinking. We need a system of continuing professional development that brings together the worlds of practice and research. We need more forums, like the NRDC or Adults Learning Mathematics at their best, where research can learn from practice, and practitioners from research.

## 'Was the research to back up the government's aims with some fine-tuning? But what if it had major criticisms? Would they be noticed or ignored?'

These questions come from an article written by one of us mid-project (Baxter 2003). We did have major criticisms: as well as challenging what measurement might mean, the research showed us that what the government thought adults wanted out of numeracy education was not what many of our students thought they wanted. Our report critiques some of the assumptions and content of the adult numeracy core curriculum (DfES & Basic Skills Agency 2001).

We fear the report may be ignored, by policymakers if not researchers. Inevitably, the collection of data, analysis, reporting and subsequent use of this sort of research takes a very long time. Meanwhile things at the 'whiteboard face' move very quickly. As we write, there are moves to link funding with achievements in the national test, further tying students and teachers to a curriculum, and forms of testing, which we found in some respects limiting. The 'Move On' initiative (DfES 2005) has now produced many (11, at last count) paper-based and electronic practice tests and it is hard not to believe that this will lead to students being prepared for tests (and thus helping to achieve government targets, though in the short term only), rather than being supported to explore and develop the full range of numeracy topics and concepts in the core curriculum – and beyond, of course – with particular effect on the measurement section of the curriculum.

One answer to the drive towards 'achievements' is to assess students early and often – every term. For that reason teachers in the college in which we developed a new scheme of work, integrating work on measures throughout the course, are being pushed into making sure that they teach a particular set of topics in a particular time frame. In a parallel move, they are strongly encouraged to use the Skills for Life materials (DfES). Topics then have to be taught in a particular order, undermining the revisiting of topics that we proposed. The scheme of work had been revised in the light of experience over the last two years, but may now be dropped. More generally, prescriptive training sessions push us away from student-led work.

It seems likely that what would be expected to be the most substantial and lasting outcomes of our project will have little impact on day-to-day numeracy teaching and learning. Our project has made a significant contribution to a surprisingly under-researched field – but we find the links between research and practice to be weak and easily broken. Far from supporting the development of a culture linking research and practice within workplaces, as the NRDC's programme of teacher research aimed to do, we have found it difficult to sustain our own involvement in research or to implement some of the changes we proposed ourselves, and while students and teachers have been positive about the project's work, we cannot claim to have influenced practice beyond our own.

But some of our work is accessible and useful (we hope) to practitioners. It is the production of the website materials that gives us, as practitioners, the greatest satisfaction. We tried to address the need for practical work on measures and encourage placing measurement at the centre of all number activities to give students regular opportunities to become familiar and more confident with measuring instruments, units and estimation skills. Teachers need materials that they can easily adapt for their own teaching contexts. We have produced them around problem-solving activities; we hope they will help teachers meet the demands of their managers while also supporting discussion, collaborative work and critical thinking among students. Alongside the teaching materials are other materials to support debate: interview and classroom transcripts showing students arguing passionately for and against aspects of numeracy education and discussing their own education and their use of measures outside the classroom; examples of particularly awful examination questions; word problems of different sorts; reading materials on the history of measures; images ... All these can be adapted for teachers and students to use as they want.

## Recognizing teachers' research

As far as we know, our report is one of the most substantial studies of teaching and learning measures available to mathematics teachers (our review of relevant research will be published with the project's final report). Our published writing has almost all centred on the project's research, both findings and problems. This chapter has been instead about the experience of being a teacher–researcher, and we want to use the opportunity to raise questions about how people read what we write. Nearly all our publications are by 'Baxter et al.'. We have been asked why, by research and development workers who assume the researcher is the main writer. For an article in conference proceedings published on the web, the editors used the researcher's name for the hyperlink, though a teacher was the lead author; when challenged, they said the researcher's name was better known (Baxter et al. 2004). Similarly, an edited extract from the final report (which is by the whole team, in alphabetical order but with the project director named last) appeared under the names of the project director and researcher (Coben and Tomlin 2005), despite our listing all the names. So it is worth describing how this chapter was written. The editors sought to include practitioner perspectives and asked around for suggestions. Our project director checked with us, the editors agreed, and here we are. The researcher drafted an outline, and the teacher–researchers wrote individual contributions. We found that there was a good deal of common ground, and decided to write with a collective voice. We had not written anything relating to some parts of the draft outline, and we missed those out. What you have read is based on sorting, checking, re-ordering and cutting duplication in the original texts, and changing *I* to *we*.

# References

Baker, E., Holder, D., Leddy, E., Tomlin, A. and Coben, D. (2003) 'Teacher research into adult numeracy: exploring the moorland (and the planetary system, the building site and the sky with clouds)' in Coben, D. (ed.) *What Counts as Evidence for What Purposes in Research in Adult Literacy, Numeracy and ESOL? Papers from the first NRDC International Conference.* Nottingham: NRDC with University of Nottingham: 128–35.

Baxter, M. (2003) 'More questions than answers'. *Adults Learning*, 15(2): 27.

Baxter, M., Leddy, E., Richards, L., Tomlin, A., Wresniwiro, T. and Coben, D. (2004) 'Teaching and learning measurement in basic numeracy courses: students' values, government's measures and the gap between them', 10th International Congress on Mathematical Education (ICME-10), downloadable from www.icme-10.dk (accessed 1 August 2004).

Baxter, M., Leddy, E., Richards, L., Tomlin, A., Wresniwiro, T. and Coben, D. (forthcoming) *'Measurement Wasn't Taught When They Built the Pyramids': The Report of the Teaching and Learning Common*

*Measures Project*. London: National Research and Development Centre for Adult Literacy and Numeracy, Institute of Education, University of London.

Baxter, M., Leddy, E., Richards, L., Wresniwiro, T., Tomlin, A. and Coben, D. (2003) 'Where is the mathematics in measurement?' in Maaß, J. and Schlöglmann, W. (eds) *Learning Mathematics to Live and Work in our World. Proceedings of the 10th International Conference on Adults Learning Mathematics*, Strobl, Austria: Universitätsverlag Rudolf Trauner: 176–82.

Coben, D. and Tomlin, A. (2005) 'Measuring change: "It's nothing to do with pottery, it's only got to do with maths" '. *Reflect*, (3): 18–19.

DfES (n.d.) 'Skills for life learning materials: numeracy', Department for Education and Skills/Adult Basic Skills Strategy Unit, downloadable from www.dfes.gov.uk/readwriteplus/LearningMaterialsNumeracy (accessed 29 July 2005).

DfES (2005) 'Move On practice tests', Department for Education and Skills/Adult Basic Skills Strategy Unit, downloadable from www.dfes.gov.uk/readwriteplus/Publications (accessed 29 July 2005).

DfES & Basic Skills Agency (2001) 'Adult Numeracy Core Curriculum,' Basic Skills Agency, downloadable from www.basic-skills.co.uk (accessed 1 September 2003).

# Section Four
## Measuring and Assessing Adult Literacy, Numeracy and Language

# 11 Education For All: The Globalization of Learning Targets

*Harvey Goldstein*

## Introduction

At its conference in Jomtien in 1990, and reaffirmed in Dakar in 2000, UNESCO adopted the declaration on 'Education For All' (EFA) that has subsequently become one of its major programmes with implementation plans at least up to the year 2015. (Full details can be found at www.unesco.org/efa.) The basic aims, set out in six goals, encourage all countries, but especially those in the developing world, to implement policies resulting in certain basic educational 'standards'. These are linked directly to other concerns including economic progress and health via a stated belief in the necessity of basic education as a foundation for satisfactory progress in these other areas. A particular emphasis is on access to primary education with the eradication of gender differences and those based on class and ethnic status. There is also a concern with adult literacy. An implementation programme is being developed, in conjunction with individual countries and regional and international organizations such as the World Bank and certain NGOs.

In order to focus its activities EFA has set up targets for achieving its aims by certain dates and the present versions of these were agreed at the Dakar meeting. Thus, for example, it is intended that by 2015 'all children ... will have access to and complete free and compulsory primary education of good quality' and by 2015 there will be 'a 50 per cent improvement in levels of adult literacy'. In this chapter, I look closely at these targets, their epistomological status, and some of the consequences of pursuing them. My intention is not to provide a general critique of the programme's aims, which are widely accepted, but rather to explore ways in which the pursuit of particular kinds of target could undermine these same aims. In particular, I will focus on the 'learning targets' such as those concerned with adult literacy and children's achievements. My main thesis is concerned with the distorting effects that 'high-stakes' target setting can lead to, by encouraging individuals to adapt their behaviour in order to maximize perceived rewards; viewed as a rational response to external pressures and for which there is now a body of research evidence derived from existing educational systems, notably in England and the United States. Other targets, for example concerned with enrolments, may also be subject to the same effects, but will generally have less direct effect on the learning process itself, and I will not discuss these.

## Measuring targets

The sixth Dakar goal refers to 'recognized and measurable learning outcomes' being 'achieved by all'. There is, however, no indication of the problematic nature of such measurements and no clearly set out description of what form the relevant assessments might take. The goal of obtaining a 50 percent improvement in adult literacy similarly lacks detail. Responsibility for setting up the necessary instruments and implementing them appears to have been assigned to UNESCO's statistics division based in Montreal. I shall first look at existing evidence on the measurement of adult literacy and then at the issue of targets for primary schoolchildren.

The most recent, and best studied, literacy survey is the International Adult Literacy Survey (IALS) that represents the collaboration of a number of countries that agreed to cooperatively investigate adult literacy on an international basis. The main findings are published in a report (OECD 1997) and there is also a technical report (Murray, Kirsch and Jenkins 1998). Nine countries initially took part, five EU member countries (France, Germany, Ireland, the Netherlands and Sweden) together with the USA, Canada, Poland and Switzerland.

A draft report of the results of the IALS in December 1995 revealed concerns about the comparability and reliability of the data, and the methodological and operational differences between the various countries. In particular, France withdrew from the reporting stage of the study and the European Commission instigated a study, including a reanalysis, of the EU dimension of IALS. The results from that investigation are reported elsewhere (Carey 2000). The ostensible aim of IALS was to provide a comparison of levels of 'prose', 'document' and 'quantitative' literacy among the countries involved using the same measuring instrument that would yield equivalent interpretations in the different cultures and different languages. Respondents, about 3,000 in each country, were tested in their homes. Each participant responded to one booklet which contained items of each literacy type and there were seven different booklet versions, which were rotated.

The reanalysis identified several problematic aspects of IALS, and by implication all such attempts at international comparisons (Blum, Goldstein and Guerin-Pace 2001), including attempts to set common international targets. In these comparisons, the dominant paradigm is that of a common measuring instrument that allows 'comparable' scores to be obtained from individuals in different educational systems. This operates through a process of translation and certain psychometric scaling techniques.

The first issue concerns the problems of translation and cultural specificity. As Blum et al. (2001) point out, there are some things that are culturally or educationally specific so that exact translations are impossible, and in many cases it is not possible to predict in advance which these items are. If a measuring instrument is restricted only to those items for which we might assume there are no locally specific differences, there is then a real question about whether such an instrument is measuring anything useful. To illustrate their point, Blum et al. (2001) give several examples. One of these concerns weather charts presented to respondents in a particular format which is more familiar in some countries than in others. Other examples are concerned with the ways in which particular languages embody linguistic structures that favour certain kinds of question wording. Through a reanalysis of data they demonstrate how the actual IALS items produced biased responses in particular cases. One example that illustrates the subtlety of cultural bias is worth repeating. The task required respondents to work out which were comedies in a review covering four films. In two of these reviews, in both English and French, the term 'comedy' appears, which makes the question easy. In France, however, they find that many interviewees gave as their answer a third film which from the description is obviously not a comedy. The only possible explanation is the presence in that film of the actor Michel Blanc, who is well known in France for his roles in many comedies but is little known abroad. Here, association predominated in the answering process to the detriment of careful reading of the reviews.

The second issue concerns the ways in which, for each of the three aspects of literacy a single score was derived from test item responses using psychometric techniques based on the assumption of a single underlying 'dimension'. As is typically done in international comparative studies, little attempt is made to explore the existence of more than one underlying dimension, despite evidence (see Goldstein and Browne 2003 for an example) that such dimensions do exist. Blum et al. (2001) point out that the psychometric scaling used tends to remove items from the final test instrument that do not 'fit' the unidimensionality assumption. They point out that the initial *balance* of items representing different dimensions therefore determines crucially what the final test actually measures and that this distorts interpretations. Nevertheless, having just a single dimension does allow a simple rank ordering of countries and the subsequent publication of international 'league tables'. Thus, the political requirement is satisfied by the application of a particular technical (psychometric) model.

The third issue, which is especially pertinent for EFA, is how literacy levels are defined. IALS, for example, uses a complicated series of five 'levels' from basic to advanced. Blum et al. (2001) demonstrate that there are alternative, and arguably equally valid, alternative formulations that lead to very different views about the 'problem' of low literacy levels. For example, Blum et al. (2001) investigate the use of a measure of literacy level based on the 'best' response given by a respondent rather than the 'average' response. Distributions of literacy level, using this measure, are completely different from the IALS distributions. Using the IALS measure, 65 percent of French interviewees with non-imputed scores have a prose literacy level of 1 or 2 (the lowest levels) while for a measure based on the best response, the proportion falls to 5 percent. For Great Britain, the proportions are respectively 48 percent at level 1 or 2 using the IALS measure, and 3 percent at the same level using the alternative measure. Thus the EFA goal of improving literacy by 50 percent is strictly meaningless unless a particular definition is adopted and justified. Indeed, using the Blum et al. (2001) alternative measure with the above values it would also be somewhat absurd. The failure of EFA to recognize and articulate this issue suggests that the stated aim has more in common with a political slogan than a scientifically based aspiration.

## Targets, high stakes and teaching to the test

Experience within existing educational systems shows that an emphasis on numerical learning targets can be dysfunctional. My argument is that similar considerations will apply internationally. In particular, that any rise in test scores should not be confused with a rise in learning achievement as opposed to test-taking performance.

In England a system of defined achievement targets for children at different ages was set up by the 1997 New Labour government. Evidence has accumulated that while there has been a general rise in actual test score levels in those aspects of the curriculum tested and in public examination results, highly dysfunctional consequences have emerged. One of these is the tendency to demotivate pupils and increase their test anxiety, especially among low achievers (Harlen and Crick 2002).

Teachers also feel that their professionalism is undermined including their capacity for creative innovation. Radnor (2002) summarizes the research evidence. One result of the controversy over this issue is that the devolved administrations of Scotland, Wales and Northern Ireland have all decided to abolish the publication of league tables. Interestingly enough, the obsession with numerical targets eventually created serious problems for government ministers. Thus Stephen Byers, then School Standards Minister, in January 1998 claimed that 57 percent (in 1996 for English for 11 year olds) 'will not do – that is why we have set a target of 80% by 2002'. It turned out to be 75 percent, although by then Byers had been moved elsewhere. The Secretary of State at the time, David Blunkett, in fact, staked his job on achieving such targets, but sensibly transferred departments before having to confess to failure. His successor as Secretary of State, Estelle Morris, was a party to the original claim and she resigned in 2002, at least partly, because the target was not reached. At the end of 2002 the government admitted that many of its earlier targets had been missed (DfES 2002). These were almost all learning targets and included targets for examinations at 16 and 19 years as well as those for younger students.

The second source of evidence on this issue comes from the USA where there is gathering evidence that 'high-stakes' testing systems that reward schools or teachers on the basis of their pupils test scores can certainly improve test scores but may have no effect on learning that is assessed independently of those tests. In the state of Texas, under former governor, George Bush, a very high-profile testing programme was instituted in 1990 for grades 3 to 10 in Texas schools. The results are used to rank schools in league tables and certain funds are allocated on the basis of the test results. Over the 1990s very large gains in student test scores were observed, and certain ethnic minority differences were reduced. Dubbed the 'Texas miracle' these results have been used as a justification for such testing programmes involving rewards given to schools for performance on the tests.

The most important manifestation of this trend in the United States is the 'No Child Left Behind' Federal education act of 2001 (www. nochildleftbehind.gov/) which mandates testing of all school pupils in grades 3 to 8 and publication of results in league table form. In one important respect it goes further than legislation in England by giving parents the right to transfer a child from a low-scoring school to a higher scoring one. There has been some strong opposition to this act from teacher unions among others (see, for example, www.nea.org).

Researchers from the RAND corporation (the report is downloadable from www.epaa.asu.edu/epaa/v8n49/) have compared the results of the intensive testing programme in Texas with results obtained from a national testing programme, the National Assessment of Educational Progress (NAEP) that is carried out over the whole of the USA. What they found was that for mathematics and reading, compared to the rest of the USA the comparative gain in test scores over time of the Texas students on the national test was much less than that implied by the Texas test scores and in some cases no different at all from changes found in the USA as a whole. Moreover, the ethnic results from NAEP showed that, if anything, in Texas the differences were increasing rather than decreasing. The researchers conclude that the concentration on preparation for the Texas state tests may be hindering an all-round development of mathematics and reading skills, especially for minority students. In both England and Texas, we see evidence that when learning outcomes are made the focus of targets, those who are affected will change their behaviour so as to maximize their 'results', even where this is dysfunctional in educational terms. At the international level it would not be surprising if we witnessed similar kinds of behaviour where the curriculum and educational infrastructures were manipulated to maximize performance on the international performance measures; whatever the deleterious side effects this might produce.

## Failure to meet the targets

While UNESCO has published lists of countries that it expects may miss the principal targets, little has been said about the consequences of so doing. If targets are to be meaningful then some kind of sanction has to be in place for those who fail to meet them. In both England and Texas, these are clearly spelt out in terms of withholding resources or even closing down institutions.

In a strategy document (UNESCO 2002) it is stated that 'governments would demonstrate their commitment to education through efforts to transform their education systems, in response to which external partners would provide financial and technical support in a transparent, predictable and flexible manner' (p. 38). One of these partners is the World Bank, which refers to the 'aid-worthiness' of countries (p. 36) and also to the target requirements in order for countries to 'receive significant increases in external financing and technical support' (p. 37). It seems, therefore, that the targets are to be taken seriously and that the stakes are high in terms of aid and other support. This is just the situation therefore where one might expect the most 'at risk', for example, poorest countries, to be tempted into 'gaming' in order to maximize perceived external rewards.

The linking of aid to achievement of targets has already begun. In

April 2002 the World Bank agreed a 'fast track initiative' (FTI) for 'high-risk' countries (EFA Global Monitoring Report 2002; World Bank 2002). Under this, selected countries receive aid in return for achieving certain 'policy reforms'. These are associated with each country's 'macroeconomic, structural and social policies and programmes to promote growth and reduce poverty' which are developed along with international agencies such as the World Bank and IMF. It seems likely that the actual achievement of the targets will be linked closely to grants or loans and that the 'reform' of systems along particular lines will become a prerequisite for many countries.

The issue of providing technical support is also of some concern, since EFA does not specify how this will be done, or even what it means. Since, however, EFA involves both curriculum change and intensive assessment it seems likely that international bodies will be invited to provide such support. Thus, curriculum development bodies, testing and examination bodies and textbook publishers are all likely players and these almost inevitably will be those with the most international experience. Thus, globally active organizations such as Educational Testing Service (Princeton, USA), University of Cambridge Local Examinations Syndicate (UCLES, Cambridge, England), CITO (Arnhem, the Netherlands), NFER-Nelson (London, England), and the Australian Council for Educational Research (ACER, Melbourne, Australia) may be expected to become a part of the EFA programme. Given the high level of technical expertise required to develop curriculum materials, and especially to construct suitable measuring instruments, we may also expect the direction taken by EFA to reflect, in part, the global interests of such corporations. Some of them are also closely involved with the OECD, sponsors of IALS, and increasingly becoming involved in international performance comparisons such as PISA (OECD 2001 download from www.pisa.oecd.org).

The operating rules in the General Agreement on Trade in Services (GATS), (see www.gats-info.eu.int/), will make it much easier than before for these global corporations to establish their presence in local situations where there is little in the way of established expertise. They will be able to argue, for example, that they possess the psychometric methodology that is required to implement testing regimes. To challenge this countries may be able to appeal, but such appeals will undoubtedly be judged by 'experts' who may well have links with, and who anyway can be expected to share the same assumptions and expertise as, the corporations themselves.

## Conclusion

Given the deficiencies identified in the EFA targets, two important questions arise. The first is why the programme has advanced so far without serious attempts to deal with these problems. The second is whether it is possible to pursue the general aims of EFA without resorting to 'targets'.

The obsession of EFA with achieving specific learning targets seems to reflect a similar set of concerns within certain national education systems, as has been indicated with examples from England and the United States. Within such systems the imposition of targets for institutions or school authorities can be viewed as an effective means of centralized control (Radnor 2002), even within the rhetoric of diversity and local decision making. At the international level, even if unintended, the eventual outcome of pursuing EFA targets may well be an increasing control of individual systems by institutions such as the World Bank or aid agencies, supported by global testing corporations. The current designation of certain developing countries as unlikely to achieve the existing targets may not only lead to demoralization in those countries, it may also allow the imposition from outside of systemic reforms under the heading of 'remedies' to put those countries 'on track'. I have only been able to outline some of the forms this might take and further systematic analysis and understanding of the processes at work would be useful.

If we return to the general aims of EFA, and if we abandon learning target setting because of all the problems I have outlined, what then? If we accept the broad aims of EFA, to raise adult literacy levels and to raise quality and participation in primary schooling, then the really important issues are not those concerned with devising specific targets but those to do with the optimum ways in which these aims can be achieved. This implies that we need to find those alternative forms of delivery, curriculum design, pedagogy, financial incentives, etc. that work best *within each country*. Each educational system can develop different criteria for assessing quality, enrolment, and so on and instead of monitoring progress towards an essentially artificial set of targets EFA could concentrate the resources that it is able to mobilize towards obtaining the necessary understandings of the dynamics of each system. This would then allow constructive policies to be implemented. The emphasis would be on the local context and culture, within which those with local knowledge can construct their own aims rather than rely on common yardsticks implemented from a global perspective.

Such a change would seem to run counter to the current orientation within UNESCO, which appears to derive from official philosophies of target setting and centrally determined 'benchmarks' that have prevailed within certain parts of the Anglophone world since at least the mid-1980s. Nevertheless, from the perspective of those countries identified as likely to fail to meet current targets, a locally contextualized perspective would seem to offer more potential for improvement. It is, after all, just those countries that are in most need of help.

*Acknowledgements*: This chapter first appeared in *Comparative Education* (2004) 40: 7–14 and is reproduced with the permission of the publishers, Taylor & Francis.

# References

Blum, A., Goldstein, H. and Guerin-Pace, F. (2001) 'International adult literacy survey (IALS): an analysis of international comparisons of adult literacy'. *Assessment in Education*, 8: 225–46.

Carey, S. (2000) *Measuring Adult Literacy – The International Adult Literacy Survey in the European Context*. London: Office for National Statistics.

DfES (2002) *Autumn Performance Report*. London: Department for Education and Skills. Also downloadable from www.dfes.gov.uk.

EFA Global Monitoring Report (2002) *Is the World on Track?* Paris [Also downloadable from www.unesco.org/education/efa/monitoring/monitoring_2002.shtml.]

Federal Education Act (2001) 'No child left behind', downloadable from www.nochildleftbehind.gov/.

Goldstein, H. and Browne, W. (2003) 'Multilevel factor analysis models for continuous and discrete data' in Olivares, A. (ed.) *Advanced Psychometrics. A Festschrift to Roderick P. McDonald*. Mahwah, NJ: Lawrence Erlbaum Associates, Inc.

Harlen, W. and Crick, R.D. (2002) *A Systematic Review of the Impact of Summative Assessment and Tests on Students' Motivation for Learning*. London: EPPI Centre, Institute of Education.

Murray, T.S., Kirsch, I.S. and Jenkins, L.B. (1998) *Adult Literacy in OECD Countries*. Washington, DC: National Center for Education Statistics.

OECD (1997) *Literacy Skills for the Knowledge Society*. Paris: OECD.

OECD (2001) *Knowledge and Skills for Life: First Results from Programme for International Student Assessment*. Paris: OECD. [Also downloadable from www.pisa.oecd.org.]

Radnor, H. (2002) 'World class education in England: a possibility?'. *Research Intelligence*, 81: 12–21.

UNESCO (2002) *Education for All: An International Strategy to put the Dakar Framework for Action on Education for All into Operation*. Paris: UNESCO. [Also downloadable from www.unesco.org/efa.]

World Bank (2002) 'Financing of first group of countries on education fast track', downloadable from www1.worldbank.org/education/adultoutreach/index.efa.asp.

# 12  Tests and Ptarmigan[1]

*Peter Lavender*

The ptarmigan is a kind of grouse living in alpine and arctic tundra areas throughout the northern hemisphere. They have feathered toes for moving across the top of the snow. Ptarmigan drag their feet in soft snow. Their beautifully adapted feet inadvertently make it easier for huntsmen to see their prints. A series of snare loops are tied into a long line, and the loops are placed flat on the ground around a favourite thicket of willows. Birds step into the loops, drag their feet forward – and are caught (Aniskowicz 1994).

Willow Ptarmigan
© R.T. Wallen

---

[1] This chapter is based on a longer one published in Lavender, P., Derrick, J. and Brooks, B. (2004) *Testing, Testing ... 1, 2, 3*. Leicester: NIACE.

## Overview

This chapter is mainly about government targets and national tests in relation to the national 'adult basic skills strategy' in England.[2] It is also about how the best of intentions can lead to disaster. Like the ptarmigan's feet, national targets have been designed for the best of reasons but there are unintended consequences and some poor effects. I call this the 'ptarmigan effect'.

## The story so far

It has been argued elsewhere (Lavender, Derrick and Brooks 2004) that the Skills for Life strategy in England differs from the recommendations of the report by Sir Claus Moser, *A Fresh Start* (Moser 1999), in two important respects. First, the strategy has moved away from the recommendation that there should be a relationship to the national target for increasing participation in basic skills programmes as set out in *The Learning Age* (DfEE 1998) and that it should be related to levels of functional literacy or numeracy skills in the adult population. In other words, the proposal was to have a participation target to raise skill levels of the population as a whole. What we have now is a target related to how many people pass a test, with the suggestion that somehow this tells us the number of people who have 'progressed one level'.

Second, the committee's intention (in recommendation 16) was that literacy and numeracy qualifications would be assessed by coursework, test or a mixture of both. It did not state that an end test should be the exclusive form of assessment. The strategy is very much about certification and this has become more urgent in the minds of both providers and policymakers. We have now passed the first milestone of 750,000 adults achieving national certificates by 2004; the next is now in view, to help 1.5 million achieve the same by 2007. The new focus is for the population to become qualified, to improve skills up to and including level 2. There had been earlier warnings about certification becoming the dominant focus in the Moser Report:

> All methods of assessment are open to abuse and some have been abused in the past. The funding methodology of various funding bodies has over-encouraged programme providers to

[2] This chapter is entirely about policy in *England*, even though the word 'national' may be used.

get people through the qualification. Coaching – or insuffi-
ciently rigorous standards in assessment of coursework – has
been a problem. Similarly some programmes have 'taught the
test'; people have sometimes passed specific entry tests for very
specific occupations in this inadequate way. (Moser 1999:
10.25)

## National public sector agreement (PSA) targets

Tests as a proxy for achievement are here to stay, not least because of the
way in which the national PSA target for adult basic skills is to be
measured. A long way from the Moser Committee's recommendations,
the adult basic skills targets are related only to the achievement of
national qualifications in basic skills and key skills at levels 1 and 2 and
adults achieving English and mathematics GCSE. In 2003 the Secretary
of State for Education and Skills, Charles Clarke, referred to the
'formidable targets' in basic skills. Closely linked is the 'record spending'
across government of £1.6 billion over three years.[3] It is not clear how
the figure is arrived at given the activity in every department.
Nevertheless it is a substantial amount[4] and without it we would not
have this unprecedented spending on adult learning. As Jane Mace puts
it: 'And we agree that we are glad. After so long at the margins, at last
there is a feeling that the job of providing fulfilling adult basic education
is moving centre stage' (Mace 2002).

The national target brings with it substantial opportunities for
potential learners, for providers and for widening participation. The link
between funding and the PSA target is key to understanding the
conundrum about basic skills qualifications. PSA targets are about
measurement and improvement. Just counting numbers of learners
involved would not indicate any progress being made: so the government
has to find another quantitative measure. But does the achieving of these
qualifications ('national test') indicate that learners are making progress?
Clarke said that he wanted '750,000 adults to improve their literacy,
language and numeracy skills by 2004'. The best that could be promised is
that many of these learners were indeed making progress, as well as
passing tests, but there is no assurance that this is so and no causal link
between progress made and the numbers passing tests – especially when

---

[3] DfES 2003, Foreword.
[4] It contrasts interestingly with the £10 billion that 'poor literacy, language and
numeracy skills are estimated to cost the country' Foreword, ibid.

anyone can take the test on line. All will depend on the quality assurance processes – inspection, strategic area review, self-assessment – together with the expectations on all providers mentioned above. The achievement of the PSA target, then, depends not on everyone learning, not on their commitment to learning, not even on the progress measured in their individual learning plan, but on the achievement of those learners who pass the national test. And it is possible to count only one of these qualifications – passing a level 2 qualification straight after level 1 will not count. It is imperfect but it is what we have got. Not much harm there, except perhaps that it will underestimate by a very long way the real achievement and participation of learners such as those at pre-entry and entry level, and there is the risk, posed by the Moser Committee, of the test corrupting the curriculum in some way.

## Tests, qualifications and funding

The strategy and the PSA target has an unhelpful side effect on the national basic skills qualifications; exactly that predicted by the Moser Committee. The Learning and Skills Council funding methodology is starting to 'over-encourage programme providers to get people through the qualification' (Moser 1999: 10.25). Similarly, some programmes have 'taught the test', and some local offices of the Learning and Skills Council are threatening to fund only provision in which learners are to take the test. All local LSCs have a target to meet, set by the LSC as a proportion of the 2004 national target. Consider this guidance from the Learning and Skills Council: 'Local LSCs are now rightly concerned to move a significantly greater amount of their providers' literacy, language and numeracy provision to that which counts towards their achieve-ment target' (DfES/LSC 2003).

Any provision for literacy, language or numeracy based on the national standards and not leading to an approved, national qualifica-tion is defined as 'other provision'. No expansion of 'other provision' can happen without 'early' discussion with an education and training provider's local LSC (DfES/LSC 2003: 2) and 'other' provision is discretionary – each local LSC can decide when and how much to allow. Providers are also reminded that the funding of qualifications 'approved for inclusion in the National Qualifications Framework (NQF) is a key priority in order to meet its challenging basic skills and level 2 and 3 targets' (DfES/LSC 2003: 2). The full text of the fact sheet issued by the LSC and DfES together allows for a little more flexibility than is immediately apparent from these points. 'Other' provision is intended to be used to encourage those not ready for a qualification or where the 'main purpose of provision is to widen participation' (DfES/LSC 2003: 4). However, the limitations attached to 'other' basic skills provision is given heavy emphasis: 'learners' abilities should not be underestimated, and if it later becomes apparent that the learner could gain a qualification, providers should take action to transfer them to qualification-bearing learning' (DfES/LSC 2003: 2, 4).

The tone is clear. It would be unusual for learners to be taking a basic skills course and not do a qualification, except where the purpose of the course is to 'widen participation'. Any course not offering a qualification might prove hard to defend during an inspection or audit. And the qualifications, as I have said, depend on an end test, even at entry level. At the time of writing (November 2005) the LSC has announced that it will favour the funding of provision that leads to a qualification and reduce the funding of provision that does not (LSC 2005).

But are the tests inadequate? Jay Derrick argues (Lavender et al. 2004) that they are no better or worse than any other summative assessment of their kind. They do what tests with no context will always do: provide a rough measure of some reading or maths levels. However, this is a long way from the good practice emphasized by the government in *Focus on Delivery to 2007* where: 'Learners can ... expect to have a teacher who gives regular, positive, recorded feedback, and who is able to use a full range of teaching approaches, from group work, to one-to-one and online learning' (DfES 2003: 112).

The quality of the tests might improve but without a connection between the formative and summative assessment they may not help learners to 'commit to their own learning' encouraged by the strategy (DfES 2003: 112). Considering the literacy national test, Jane Mace notes:

> This is an exercise about measuring. ... But it is not a test of literacy. To call it such must be regarded as an abuse of language. This is a test not of literacy, but of reading, and of a very particular kind of reading at that. And it embodies a mistaken (and dangerous) idea that truly literate people always write alone, unaided and without mistakes, and that anyone else is lacking 'basic skills' ... it has nothing to do with the real world where people read and write. In the real world (rather than the artificial one of tests), experience and research both tell us that everyone engages in literacy within a social context, and often that context implies cooperation, not solitary testing. (Mace 2002)

Without a good-quality test (and maybe they are as good as they can be given the early stage of their development), with the pressure of a funding method, and with priorities lying with one form of measuring achievement, what can be done to offer good-quality 'other' provision that puts learners first?

## Tests, national targets and social inclusion

'Other' provision simply means literacy, language and numeracy provision that does not lead to an 'approved' qualification. Its purpose is to widen participation or form part of the social inclusion agenda. *The Learning Curve* (ODPM 2002) suggests 'what works' in neighbourhoods in order to reduce social exclusion. It is part of the comprehensive learning and development strategy for neighbourhood renewal. Encouragingly, *The Learning Curve* does not try to say that one size fits all – different people need different learning tools that encompass more than formal training. The report identifies closely interrelated problems: lack of adequate childcare facilities and pre-school learning; poor school attendance; low pupil/parent expectations; high rates of school exclusion; low levels of educational achievement; low levels of participation and qualifications; and low levels of literacy and numeracy among adults (ODPM 2002: 6). Intervention suggestions include 'provision for adult education and lifelong learning' (note the 'integrated' model of provision). To widen adults' participation in learning, it is suggested, requires:

> effective information, advice and guidance (IAG) [which] can make a major contribution. ... Gaps in basic skills ... need to be addressed with some tact and imagination. ... Some projects have found it more productive to use a 'gateway' course – eg on ITC skills – as a means of providing people with a comfortable environment in which to come forward. Community-based provision is particularly important here. (ODPM 2002: 8)

How different in tone from the guidance on recording adult literacy, language and numeracy provision! *The Learning Curve* is one of many publications on what works in relation to widening participation. If the models of provision are flexible enough for those hardest to reach, why can we not use such models for everyone else? If we make it right for these learners and potential learners, might we not get it right for all, and might we not have a better chance of meeting those targets?

Every year surveys tell us that a significant minority of adults do not perceive that they have participated in learning since they left school, and a huge majority of these say they have no intention of doing so in the future (Sargant 2000). The numbers of adults participating in learning remains relatively unchanged year after year. Those most advantaged by initial education, wealth, good health, and social class, do more. Those with least purchase on the system do the least learning after leaving school. It has been observed many times that the suggestion of a national test is not a motivator for adults who are not traditional participants in adult learning. In themselves, the tests will not widen participation unless they bring with them some kind of opportunity perceived by the individual to be of value.

What is needed is a way of measuring achievement which motivates and sustains learners in their commitment to their own learning (DfES 2003: 112). We need to link together the good practice which learners can expect in the use of formative assessment with summative assessment and a valued qualification. The assessment needs to be in a context recognizable to the learner, as the government suggests (DfES 2003: 112), and in tune with the learners' interests and requirements. To reduce the risk of the ptarmigan effect – of twisting the curriculum and the funding of provision out of shape – the government could usefully continue to focus on the numbers of people actually learning as well as those achieving qualifications. Counting the numbers involved in learning would give a guide to the scale of the response from the public. If the government needs a picture of progress towards the PSA or Moser Committee's targets then a measurement of levels of literacy and numeracy in the population could be determined by regular omnibus survey. This is done for the adult participation data. Together, these figures could be more useful for Treasury funding purposes and offer less risk that only certain kinds of learning in literacy, language or numeracy is regarded as valid.

Measuring in more than one way allows for a more rounded picture. If we don't do this we can fall into the trap of thinking that a simple figure can tell us answers about progress, participation, success and achievement. It can't. As Charles Handy noted in *The Empty Raincoat*, the Macnamara Fallacy suggests that:

> The first step is to measure whatever can be easily measured. This is OK as far as it goes. The second step is to disregard that which can't easily be measured or to give it an arbitrary quantitative value. This is artificial and misleading. The third step is to presume that what can't be measured easily really isn't important. This is blindness. The fourth step is to say that what can't be easily measured really doesn't exist. This is suicide. (Handy 1994: 219)

This was five years before the Moser Committee reported. It is clear that better and more accurate counting of one thing will do no more than measure one aspect of what is there; it won't widen participation, increase the numbers of people learning or improve the quality and effectiveness of what they learn. If the funding only values one aspect of provision, even though it might recognize 'other' kinds of motivation for learning literacy, language or numeracy, then the 'abuse' feared by the Moser Committee will become a reality. And, at the time of writing, it is already very real. Cuts in 'other' adult education provision threaten programmes that do not lead to a qualification and among them are literacy, language and numeracy (AoC 2005). In addition, some provision for adults with learning difficulties is described as being under threat unless it can be described as 'basic skills provision'. There may be many different reasons for these behaviours, not all of them rest with funders. An indicator of the Learning and Skills Council's concern about cuts in literacy, language or numeracy provision is the letter from the director of resources to colleges, which warns of significant cuts in funding for adults, although literacy, language and numeracy should be safeguarded (Russell 2005). Such cuts in funding will leave colleges with cuts to make themselves and there is some indication that this will affect any provision not directly leading to national targets, whether or not this is the LSC's intention (Kingston 2005).

## Conclusion

*A Fresh Start* (Moser 1999) recommended national targets for literacy and numeracy levels for adults. These targets were related to overall literacy/numeracy levels in the population, complemented the strategies for schools, and aimed to raise participation. The Skills for Life strategy, revised in 2003, contains targets related not to participation but to qualifications achieved by learners at levels 1 and 2. The goal was not necessarily to improve functional literacy, language and numeracy, as the Moser Committee proposed, but to improve skills and the numbers of people with qualifications up to and including level 2. The Moser Committee had recognized that qualifications based on course work and on tests were appropriate, provided that both were based on the new national adult literacy and numeracy curricula. *A Fresh Start* warned that too close a focus on qualifications can distort the curriculum. Recent government strategy documents refer only to end test qualifications as the means of valuing achievement. However, there is recognition of the importance of formative as well as summative assessment. This is not carried through to policy implementation, since local Learning and Skills Councils have been told to favour the funding of qualification-bearing courses in adult literacy, language and numeracy above those that are not. The recording of the numbers of people passing tests is only a proxy for the measurement of achievement. This recording will not in itself measure the country's progress, only individual achievement, and even then only achievement of a certain kind, since the national tests are free of context and free of any link with formative assessment. It is formative assessment that is likely to improve much of the poor quality of teaching too (Curtis 2003). The national tests do offer an easy way to create a target and draw down very welcome resources. Without them we would have made even less progress towards a lifelong learning culture.

This chapter concludes with the observation that, in themselves, the national tests will not widen participation, because they are an inflexible way of measuring individual progress and of encouraging more and different people to participate. What is needed is a balance of ways of measuring achievement available to learners, and a more flexible use of opportunities that make a link between formative and summative assessment, such that the assessment is in a context recognizable to the learner and in tune with the learners' interests and requirements. The collection of participation data, with regular national surveys on literacy levels, would give a better and more accurate national picture. This is more in tune with what the Moser Committee suggested, easier for administrators to fund, and less open to the kinds of abuse of the curriculum noted by the committee in 1999. Ptarmigan feet are perfectly constructed for what they need to do. Sadly, the simplicity of their design is also their downfall since they can be more easily tracked, and snared. So it is I think with the national targets: the shift of focus to a test caused by their adoption as a PSA target might distract attention from participation, from real measures of achievement, and from the proper learner-centred curriculum.

# References

Aniskowicz, B.T. (1994) *Hinterland Who's Who Ministry of Supply and Services*. Canada: Canadian Wildlife Service.

AoC (2005) 'Government marks adult learners' week by cutting up to 200,000 places'. Association of Colleges Press Release, 20 May.

Curtis, P. (2003) ' "Poor teaching blocking adult literacy" say inspectors'. *Guardian*, 26 September.

Department for Education and Employment (DfEE) (1998) *The Learning Age: A Renaissance for a New Britain*. London: HMSO.

Department for Education and Skills (DfES) (2003) *Skills for Life – The National Strategy for Improving Adult Literacy and Numeracy Skills: Focus on Delivery to 2007*. London: DfES Publications.

Department for Education and Skills/Learning Skills Council (DfES/LSC) (2003) Joint DfES/LSC Fact Sheet *Recording Adult Literacy Language and Numeracy ('Basic Skills') Provision*. LSC Bulletin 5, 20 March.

Handy, C. (1994) *The Empty Raincoat*. London: Hutchinson.

HMSO (1998) *The Learning Age*. London: The Stationery Office.

Kingston, P. (2005) 'Pleasure breach'. *Guardian*, 21 June.

Lavender, P., Derrick, J. and Brooks, B. (2004) *Testing, Testing ... 1, 2, 3*. London: NIACE.

LSC (2005) *Priorities for Success*. Coventry: Learning and Skills Council.

Mace, J. (2002) 'Can't someone in the real world write a proper test for literacy?' *Guardian*, 28 May.

Moser, Sir C. (1999) *A Fresh Start: Improving Literacy and Numeracy*. London: Report of the Working Group, Department for Education and Skills.

Office of the Deputy Prime Minister (ODPM) (2002) *The Learning Curve*. London: Neighbourhood Renewal Unit.

Russell, D. (2005) *FE Funding for 2005/06 Academic Year: Letter to all College Leaders Confirming the Total FE Funding Allocations for 2005/ 06*. London: Learning and Skills Council.

Sargant, N. (2000) *The Learning Divide Revisited*. London: NIACE.

# 13 Performance Measurement within Adult Literacy, Language and Numeracy: Practitioners' Perspectives

*Jay Derrick*

## Introduction

The ideas in this chapter are based on the experience of working in England as a teacher and manager in the field of adult literacy, language and numeracy education between 1975 and 2001. During that time the political and administrative context within which adult education teachers work (including teachers of adult literacy, language and numeracy) changed dramatically. Before 1992, regulation and oversight was typically very light, particularly in the adult education sector, where the majority of provision was situated. There was no standard curriculum, no regulations for the qualifications of teachers, and very little external assessment of learning. For many teachers the only formal record-keeping requirement was the maintenance of an up-to-date register of attendance, and this was primarily as a safety measure in case of fire. The Further and Higher Education Act of 1992 brought adult education in England and Wales (including adult literacy, language and numeracy) into an enlarged further education sector, and also created a national system of further education for the first time, coordinated by a national body rather than by hundreds of local authorities, and within a single national funding system (Green and Lucas 1999). In the mid-1990s, policy began to focus sharply on adult literacy, language and numeracy as key determinants of national prosperity and social equity (Hamilton 1996), a process intensified and accelerated by the publication of the International Adult Literacy Survey (see Fowler 2005), and leading to the launching of Skills for Life, the national strategy for adult literacy, language and numeracy in England and Wales, in 2001.

This fundamental reorganization of the post-16 sector initiated by the Conservative government in the early 1990s embodied three key organizational principles, all accepted unquestioningly by the three New Labour administrations since 1997. These are, first, that the basic purpose of all learning is the gaining of qualifications; second, that in order to achieve comparability of standards and maintain the market-ability of qualifications, assessment should largely be external; and, third, that publishing league tables of provider performance based on the number of qualifications gained is an effective way to drive up standards. The assumption is that these principles are equally valid for all settings and levels of learning, and for all types of learner. In particular they are applied to Skills for Life courses, and should be seen by policy analysts as fundamental features of it, as critical as curriculum documents and assessment materials. They reveal a powerfully positivist philosophical perspective on knowledge and on education.

These changes, both to the post-16 system as a whole, and to the regulation of adult basic education, have had a profound effect on the work of teachers and managers working within adult literacy, numeracy and language. The present chapter looks in detail at a key aspect of the new system, performance measurement, and outlines its impact on classroom practice and the management of provision for literacy, language and numeracy. It argues that the present system is an example of a 'command and control' approach to quality improvement in public service delivery (Seddon 2003). In the interests of producing comparable and consistent data for accountability and benchmarking, teachers are being deskilled, learners are being short-changed, and the public is being misled about the effectiveness or otherwise of the Skills for Life strategy. This last is because inappropriate tools are being used to gather data, and because many of the interpretations put on the data are unwarranted. The chapter concludes with a brief outline of an alternative approach, suggesting that we would be better served by a quality improvement system that accepts that the provisionality of its conclusions is inevitable, that balances the evaluative use of quantitative data with qualitative professional judgements, that nurtures public trust in such judgements, and which builds professional capacity and expertise rather than diminishing it.

## Performance measurement in adult literacy, numeracy and language

The infrastructure for performance measurement is a key feature of the new policy framework for all post-16 education and training. Diverse and incompatible arrangements for monitoring and improving quality at the level of local education authorities have been replaced by a single national system. It is characterized by national and institutional targets, the annual publishing of institutional performance measures in the form of league tables, and periodic inspections which grade providers on a five-point scale, with the results published widely. The system is applied equally to general-purpose further education colleges, local authority adult education services, national and local voluntary sector providers, and work-based learning providers. Successfully inspected providers can become 'centres of excellence', whereas unsuccessful inspections can lead to 'naming and shaming' and 'special measures', or even closure.

The stated objectives of this system are to raise performance and effectiveness across the sector. Can we be sure that it will? John Seddon (2003) describes this approach to quality improvement as the 'command and control' approach, and shows how target setting in public services often leads to lower productivity and quality of service, because staff and managers are forced to focus on delivering the immediate target rather than taking a holistic and longer term view of improving their services. Does this apply to teachers, managers and institutions providing adult literacy, language and numeracy? Do they start adapting their programmes and policies to service the targets, rather than keeping focused on the needs of learners? I believe that they do, and that this is detrimental to learners and ultimately the policy objectives Skills for Life is aiming to support. Here are two examples.

## Example 1

At the time of writing (summer 2005), skills for life courses at entry level (that is, courses for learners working below level 1 of the national qualifications framework) are being cut in many areas: funding is contracting and these entry level courses, which do not contribute to the national and regional targets, are lower priority than those at levels 1 or 2, which do. Staff who teach these courses are facing redundancy. This is in spite of the national shortage of skills for life teachers, and the very large proportion of skills for life learners who need at least some tuition at entry level.

## Example 2

Managers and teachers of skills for life courses are under heavy pressure to deliver high and improving 'achievement rates' for their organizations, whether large further education colleges with thousands of students or small community centres with a couple of dozen. The 'achievement rate' is measured by dividing the number of individual qualifications gained by learners on a course or group of courses, by the number of learners who originally enrolled for the course or courses, and expressing this as a percentage. National benchmarks are produced for each qualification, and it is essential for each provider's rate to be improving each year against this benchmark. 'Achievement rates' are 'high stakes' statistics because it is on this figure that providers are ranked in league tables published each year. This means it is not in a provider's interest to enrol a learner who for any reason might not complete the course and gain the qualification. Rather, providers who wish to move up the league tables must strive to ensure they do not enrol learners who do not complete their course or who fail to achieve their chosen qualification, even though they may be learners with the greatest social and economic need. Managers and teachers involved in course guidance and in initial diagnostic assessment spend a lot of their time figuring out how to square this circle: their options consist only in trying to organize their programmes to suit performance measurement rather than learners, or in appearing to be inefficient and/or ineffective.

Perhaps none of this would be a problem if the measurement tools and standards used by the system were perfectly fit for purpose. In that case, achievement rates would perfectly reflect the quality of teaching for the institutions concerned: social, economic and personal pressures which might lead to some learners dropping out would be distributed evenly throughout all sectors and regions; the reasons for learners not completing would be dependent on factors within teachers' control; the qualifications gained by learners would perfectly represent what they need to learn as well as what society needs them to learn; and the instruments and processes used to assess learning would be perfectly valid (that is, they would fairly assess the whole range of relevant skills, knowledge and capacity) and reliable (they would produce the same result for each learner however many times they were used).

Actually, the arrangements applying to skills for life courses satisfy none of these criteria. Reasons for learner non-completion are not well researched, but common sense tells us that they do not apply evenly to all sectors, regions, and groups of learners. Many learners leave courses for economic or family reasons: they may get a job which prevents them attending, or have to care for a sick child or elderly relative, clearly not factors the teacher can influence. There exists a range of views about the extent to which the national standards and curriculum documents reflect learners' needs, or the needs of employers – this is a deeply contested debate, which accounts for the wide range of curriculum frameworks and content descriptors adopted by different countries, even those with relatively similar socioeconomic and cultural profiles (compare for example the England and Wales standards for adult literacy, numeracy and ICT (QCA 2005) with the US *Equipped for the Future* standards (Stein 2000), or *Learning for Living* (New Zealand

Ministry of Education 2005)). Many countries, indeed, see no need for a national curriculum at all. Finally, one might think that the main skills for life assessment instruments – which are used, first, to accredit learners, second, as the key tool for performance measurement of provision and of teachers, third, to determine significant amounts of 'achievement funding' for providers for each qualification gained, and finally as the key currency for the national targets – would be unproblematic, but sadly this is not the case. The national tests for literacy at levels 1 and 2 have low 'validity' because they only assess reading and not speaking, listening or writing, which are all important sections of the national standards and curriculum for literacy. Also, they are made up of multiple-choice questions which require reading skills to understand: this reduces their reliability. As it stands, the major instrument for producing the only quantitative data for evaluating the effectiveness of the Skills for Life policy in respect of literacy, cannot be said to evaluate literacy at all, but only reading. The extent to which it can evaluate improved preparedness for employment across the population, or improved work skills, higher productivity, or lower levels of social exclusion, would be open to question even if it was a perfectly valid test in its own terms, as the national curriculum descriptors which it aims to test are in any case only a proxy for those broader social and economic objectives (finding ways to measure the real benefits of learning across the whole social field is the purpose of the Wider Benefits of Learning Research Centre: see for example Schuller et al. 2004).

Finally, to construct the league tables, which are the point of the whole system, it is necessary to rank the results of these measurements for each provider. Unfortunately, there are serious doubts about the extent to which raw achievement or even value-added data used for league tables of schools, colleges, or nation states are in fact statistically comparable, and therefore whether confident assertions can be made about the relative quality of the different institutions making provision for literacy, language and numeracy. Harvey Goldstein's chapter in this section of the book, focusing on international comparisons, argues the case in more detail. The point he makes is that the data so produced, based simply on qualifications achieved, do not by themselves provide objective evidence: they need to be interpreted. This is because of myriad social, cultural and environmental factors that continually impact on the processes through which the data are collected.

## Impact of the English performance measurement system on teaching practice

We have seen some of the ways in which the planning and provision of adult literacy, language and numeracy courses are affected by the performance measurement system applied to provider institutions over time. These effects also operate at the level of the managers of provision, and of teachers in classrooms. The counting and ranking of qualifications gained and 'achievement rates' can be carried out at any level in the system, down to individual departments, curriculum teams, and individual teachers. This is now routine in most medium and large providers, which are under continual pressure to increase the percentage achievement rate. Departments are targeted by senior management, curriculum teams are targeted by heads of department, and individual teachers are targeted by their team leaders. This level of continuous detailed scrutiny is aided by the IT-based management information systems which are now characteristic features of all medium and large educational providers (though they usually function more as mechanisms for accountability than for improving quality). This close scrutiny by senior managers, an example of how IT can be used as a 'panopticon' (Zuboff 1989) to support hierarchical management through control, is a key feature of working life as now experienced by teachers in post-16 education and training. However, it is scrutiny less of the quality of their daily professional practice, which could be a basis for improved practice through professional development, than of their rates of 'retention' (enrolled students still on the course) and achievement. This emphasis and the working culture it engenders has a powerful tendency to become internalized over time, so that teachers too come to see their sole professional objective as higher achievement rates.

The practical effects of this close scrutiny on the day-to-day practice of teachers have not yet been researched in the post-16 sector, but evidence from studies of school teachers (the monitoring system in English schools is similar) suggests that the effects are subtle but very significant. The key research study is that of Black and Wiliam (1998a, 1998b), which shows that as the political importance of achievement rates increases, then the more teachers focus their practice on summative assessment, and the less they engage in formative assessment practices, which, the research shows, are the most effective way to improve learning. These results apply more strongly to less confident learners (Harlen and Crick 2002), and it is reasonable to suppose that they will also apply to learners and teachers in the post-16 sector, and particularly to adult literacy, language and numeracy (Derrick 2004). New research is addressing these questions for the post-16 sector (see Improving

Formative Assessment in Vocational Education and Literacy, Language and Numeracy Project (www.education.ex.ac.uk/ifa/).

## Alternative approaches

Because of its fundamental dependence on the measurement of qualifications gained, the performance measurement system for post-16 education in England and Wales is inseparable from the systems for the assessment of learning, and many of the epistemological and statistical problems inherent in the first are also applicable to the second. These problems are part of a wider phenomenon implicit in the goal of *evidence-based* policymaking. No one would want to argue against the objective of basing policy on evidence rather than prejudice or whimsy. However, it is reasonable to ask about what kinds of evidence are meant. The phrase implies that if enough relevant 'hard data' are collected and analysed, policy decisions will be made tidily on the basis of certainty, although risk society analysis suggests that even 'hard data' are likely to be unreliable in a world of increasing uncertainty, unpredictability, and continual change (for example, Beck 1992). In spite of this, the most common response to the evaluation of complex systems among policymakers and civil servants has been to collect even more hard data. O'Neill (2002) suggests that this tendency in policymaking, combined with a methodological approach to evidence gathering which values numerical data over professional judgement, is a sign of a fundamental lack of trust in society, and that policies based on this approach materially contribute to further diminution of trust and social capital. She calls for an approach to policy- and decision making in which trust rather than mistrust of professionals is the norm, and for a renewed model of professional practice based on openness, integrity, accountability and awareness of the limits of certainty. In this model of quality assurance in public services, numerical data based on standardized instruments would be used alongside other kinds of evidence, including stakeholder value judgements, qualitative accounts, and appropriate expert and professional judgements, in a system which valued multiple perspectives, reflected more accurately the nature of the processes being evaluated, and, it is argued here, would produce more meaningful results. They would be more meaningful because they would be recognized by all as indicative and provisional, the product of the best knowledge and expertise available, rather than pretending to an unrealizable and misleading degree of certainty.

Preserving the myth that judgements of educational attainment have some kind of external, scientifically verified status as objective truth is unsustainable. While so many stakeholders continue to look for ways of shoring up this misperception, the system is unlikely to fulfil its full potential. In reality, giving up on the search for 'the answer' that will fix the system's problems is likely to be the first step towards a more sustainable approach to measuring educational standards (Skidmore 2003).

These arguments apply equally to the systems for performance measurement, and suggest that a 'complex systems' approach to reform of educational assessment and performance measurement is now urgent. What is needed in my view is a new approach to assessment of learning and performance measurement in adult literacy, language and numeracy which might embody the following principles:

- Literacy, numeracy and language practices are recognized as multiple, complex and dynamic, and as manifested in social relations between individuals rather than as unidimensional qualities inherent in individuals.
- Learners are recognized as the most important stakeholders in assessment and performance measurement processes.
- Assessment of learners is detached from assessment for accountability and performance measurement of teachers and institutions.
- Emphasis is placed firmly on formative assessment and this is reflected in professional development.
- Moderation is formally structured as collaborative professional development and reflective practice.
- A range of contingent evidence bases for improvements in literacy, numeracy and language are developed: the 'wider benefits of learning' (Schuller et al. 2004) are recognized and evaluated.
- Systems for assessment of learning and performance measurement are explicitly based on trust, professional judgements, and the recognition of provisionality.

In a system governed by these principles, we might expect to see a number of features absent from the present arrangements. These would include a much wider range of assessment methods and tools in use, the use of descriptive, narrative and qualitative discourses as well as quantitative and numerical data for both assessment of learning and performance evaluation, and assessment and evaluation against criteria reflecting wider, non-educational benefits of learning. Such a system would broaden the range of benefits gained by learners, contribute to building and maintaining the professional expertise of teachers, and would be more likely to raise and then maintain standards of achievement. The task facing us is to convince policymakers that outcomes as measured by such a changed system would be more reliable and of greater utility than the bleakly impoverished and misleading data sets produced by the present system.

# References

Beck, U. (1992) *Risk Society: Towards a New Modernity*. London: Sage.

Black, P. and Wiliam, D. (1998a) 'Assessment and classroom learning'. *Assessment in Education*, 5(1): 1998.

Black, P. and Wiliam, D. (1998b) *Inside the Black Box: Raising Standards through Classroom Assessment*. London: King's College.

Derrick, J. (2004) 'Making the grade: assessment and achievement in adult literacy, numeracy and language' in Lavender, P., Derrick, J. and Brooks, B. (eds) *Testing, Testing . . . 1, 2, 3*. Leicester: NIACE.

Fowler, Z. (2005) 'Politically constructing adult literacy: a case study of the Skills for Life strategy for improving adult literacy in England'. Unpublished MA thesis, London: Institute of Education.

Green, A. and Lucas, N. (1999) *FE and Lifelong Learning: Realigning the Sector for the Twenty-first Century*. London: Institute of Education Bedford Way Papers.

Hamilton, M. (1996) 'Literacy and adult basic education' in Fieldhouse, R. (ed.) *A History of Modern British Adult Education*. Leicester: NIACE.

Harlen, W. and Crick, R.D. (2002) *A Systematic Review of the Impact of Summative Assessment and Tests on Students' Motivation for Learning*. London: EPPI Centre, Institute of Education.

Improving Formative Assessment in Vocational Education and Literacy, Language and Numeracy Project, downloadable from www.education. ex.ac.uk/ifa/ (accessed 30 June 2005).

New Zealand Ministry of Education (2005) *Learning for Living/Te Ako mo Te Ora: Draft Descriptive Standards, Describing the Literacy, Language and Numeracy Competencies that Adults need to Meet the Demands of their Everyday Lives*. Wellington, New Zealand: New Zealand Ministry of Education. [Also downloadable from www.nzliteracyportal.org.nz/ download/20050307080355stds_doc.pdf (accessed 30 June 2005).]

O'Neill, O. (2002) *A Question of Trust, the 2002 Reith Lectures*. London: BBC. [Also downloadable from www.bbc.co.uk/radio4/reith2002/ (accessed 30 June 2005).]

QCA (2005) *National Standards for Adult Literacy, Numeracy and ICT.* London: The Qualifications and Curriculum Authority. [Also downloadable from www.qca.org.uk/downloads/14130_national_standards_for_adult_literacy_numeracy_ict.pdf (accessed 30 June 2005).]

Seddon, J. (2003) *Freedom from Command and Control: A Better Way to Make the Work Work.* London: Vanguard Education Ltd.

Schuller, T., Preston, J., Hammond, C., Basset-Grundy, A. and Bynner, J. (2004) *The Benefits of Learning: The Impact of Education on Health, Family Life and Social Capital.* London: Routledge Falmer.

Skidmore, P. (2003) 'Beyond measure: why educational assessment is failing the test', downloadable from http://www.demos.co.uk/catalogue/beyondmeasure/ (accessed 30 June 2005).

Stein, S. (2000) *Equipped for the Future Content Standards: What Adults Need to Know and be Able to do in the 21st Century.* Washington, DC: National Institute for Literacy. [Also downloadable from www.eff.cls.utk.edu/PDF/standards_guide.pdf (accessed 30 June 2005).]

Zuboff, S. (1989) *In the Age of the Smart Machine.* London: Basic Books.

# Section Five
## Crossing Boundaries: Facilitating Interactions

# 14 Crossing Borders – and Back Again: A Life of Building Bridges, Squaring Circles and Living Literacy as Social Practice

*Juliet Merrifield*

My work in adult education over almost 30 years has taken me back and forth between research, practice and policy-related work (as well as across the Atlantic). It's not a comfortable route, or one I'd recommend wholeheartedly, but it has been interesting. I'd like to reflect on what I've learned about crossing these borders and about how the 'literacy as social practices' approach provides a particular perspective on the domains and their boundaries.

Three ideas tie the boundary crossings together:

- The importance of 'popular knowledge' or knowledge based on experience – whether enshrined in text or not – as a counterpoint to 'official knowledge' which is usually written (but not necessarily accessible). Literacies are an expression of power relationships in society.
- We should never lose sight of the fact that learning is one of the tools with which people can change their lives, not just through individual advancement, but through social and community change. It really isn't *just* about skills or jobs (although these are important to learners too).
- The relationships between practice, research and policy are always messy and inconsistent. We often ask how knowledge from research and practice can be heard and have an impact on policy. Perhaps we shouldn't be trying to cross borders so much as mix things up, to bring research and policy into practice and vice versa.

In what follows I will try to illustrate these ideas with a few of the stories that have helped me learn them, and to ask what a social practices view of literacy contributes to their understanding.

## Popular knowledge and literacies

The first time I had a glimmer of a social practices approach to literacy was as a young teenager. I remember watching my mother having a demonstration from *her* mother of how to make a traditional North Devon 'yeast cake'. I knew that my grandmother, and most of the women in Appledore, had always made these, and that my mother had been trying to get a recipe for a long time. No recipe books seemed to include it, and attempts to get my grandmother to pass on the recipe that was in her head had not worked. So experiential learning was the plan: my mother would make the yeast cake under my grandmother's supervision, writing down the steps as she went. What I learned from this is that some things cannot be written easily. The attempt to render 'a pinch of this and handful of that, add water until it looks right' into text didn't work, and I don't remember seeing my mother try to make a yeast cake again.

It was an early experience of what, much later, I learned to call 'popular knowledge'. This is the knowledge born of experience, often passed on orally and visually, seldom expressed in text and increasingly devalued as a result. I learned to name and understood the concept more when I worked from 1977 to 1987 at the Highlander Research and Education Center in Tennessee, USA, a residential adult education centre committed to social justice. It was my first boundary crossing: from research into practice and even into policy-related work (albeit policy from the position of those affected by it rather than the policymakers).

Highlander started in the union movement of the 1930s and came of age in the civil rights movement of the 1950s and 1960s. By the time I started working there its work was mainly in poor communities of the Appalachian mountain region and I joined the research programme. We worked with community organizations and unions that were actively involved in a wide range of community issues – healthcare in rural communities, the environmental effects of strip mining, impacts of absentee ownership of the land, among others. Our goal was to get people involved in decisions that affect their lives. The educational philosophy developed by Highlander's founder, Myles Horton, paralleled Paolo Freire in many ways (Bell, Gaventa and Peters 1990). In essence, he believed that the best learning comes from action, and the greatest action is action for social justice. My partner and I, with brand new doctorates and some years of research experience between us, at first thought that we would do research *for* the groups that were fighting these battles. We soon found there were too many of them and too few of us and we started instead to teach activists in these community groups how to do their own research to support their action. It was with great excitement that we discovered that what we were doing had a name, and that there were other people doing it, mainly in the developing world but also in Canada. Since then the 'participatory action research' (PAR) movement has grown and developed much more widely.

Popular knowledge is a central concept in PAR. I came to understand it more through working with a community called Bumpass Cove, a small former mining community in a Tennessee mountain hollow that was trying to close down and then clean up a toxic waste dump at the head of the valley (Merrifield 1993). The community's knowledge challenged the assurances of the state Department of Health that all was well: residents could document children falling ill, wild animals found dead, trees and plants dying. I worked with a group who wanted to access and understand the official knowledge and to systematize community members' own knowledge. None of the group had completed high school and one woman had left school at 14 to get married; much later the two women in the group joined a local literacy programme and got their GEDs.

Using the Freedom of Information Act, the group was able to gain access to the files of the state Department of Health and together we sorted through their photocopies to track all recorded shipments into the landfill over its life. Then we used a chemical reference book, a medical reference book and a dictionary to document potential health effects of the chemicals that were known to have been dumped there, entry routes (ingestion, breathing, skin) and any safe levels that had been set for exposure in workplaces, water and air. With the incentive that came from knowing that their own and their children's health was at stake, the group was able to make sense of the challenging texts and for the first time began to feel that they had some control over information. Their literacy learning represented a power shift: they took on the experts at their own game, and were delighted to be able to challenge health department inspectors with their new knowledge. At the same time they used popular knowledge to map illegal and unreported dumping and to identify health and wildlife concerns.

In research terms, the social practices approach to literacy has taken on board very clearly the power relationships intrinsic in literacies. But we have been less clear and focused on placing literacy within a framework of 'knowing' – or epistomology. Brian Street points out in his contribution to *Powerful Literacies* that the 'new epistomological order' offers researchers and academics a role in critiquing the bases of knowledge claims and working with partners in the interests of equity and justice (Street 2001).

Practitioners, on the whole, are comfortable with starting with what learners already know and recognizing that someone who can't read and write well nevertheless may be very knowledgeable. Perhaps we could unpack further the relationship between knowledge and literacies, focusing on who knows, what they know, how it is communicated to others, and how power shapes how it is received.

From my work at Highlander in environmental and occupational health and participatory action research, I began to document ways in which power holders use the cloak of scientific knowledge to 'assure people of their own ignorance' (Merrifield 1993). These ways include to:

- defuse – often by delay, setting up a long study so that people give up
- bemuse – impress or blind them with science
- confuse – provide a gloss to assure people that official knowledge is backed with science and their own knowledge is of dubious validity.

The Bumpass Cove experience has been a crucial one for my own learning and development. Looking back it seems to make three key points:

1　It symbolizes the crossing of the border between research because something is interesting to research as a crucial part of acting on an issue. As an old union song goes, when it comes to social action 'there are no neutrals there'. In other words, this kind of research is a part of practice, not separated from it and it has a purpose and values.
2　It shows how crucial it is *both* to document popular knowledge based on experience *and* to recapture official knowledge in order to systematize, understand and act on a problem.
3　It uncovers the role of power in literacies. Written knowledge acquires some power just from being written down. The social practices approach is key to recognizing that the power of literacy is based on *who* knows and *how* they know as well as *what* they know.

## Literacy learning as a tool to change lives

The Bumpass Cove community members who learned about toxic chemicals, state government and the power of corporations had their lives changed – albeit not in ways they might have anticipated. Going 'back to school' was part of the same story for them, linked through the confidence and insights they gained as part of the community struggle.

In the early 1990s I was involved in some research for the US Congress Office of Technology Assessment that took me further in understanding the lives of literacy and language learners. Later published as *Life at the Margins* (Merrifield et al. 1997), we followed 12 people with limited literacy and/or language skills, including native English speakers, immigrants and refugees. We profiled their educational history, life story, everyday literacy and language practices and use of technologies.

Self-reliance and independence were key themes in the lives of everyone we profiled. They were all living 'at the margins' in terms of income, work (low-wage and low-skill), job security and prospects. The drive to independence meant hard work and long hours to support their families. Everyone had hopes and aspirations, for themselves and for their children.

Everyone we profiled had a history of learning, some mostly informal and others including more formal programmes. For the most part people learned what they needed to know at a particular moment in time to achieve a specific goal and then moved on. When they took part in a formal class their goals and self-assessment did not necessarily match those of their teachers. Learning had not transformed their lives in economic terms, but was part of their wider lives.

A more recent book on the *Benefits of Learning* maps out what most of us know in an informal way from our own practice: that learning carries benefits that go far beyond the economic (Schuller et al. 2004). The book addresses three forms of 'capital' that can be built through learning – human capital, social capital and identity capital – and takes us through some of the very individual ways in which people change through learning experiences.

I was particularly intrigued by the section on health and well-being. It argues the concepts of purpose (or aspirations) and perseverance (or commitment) as integral to a sense of identity. These create feedback loops through which self-esteem and self-efficacy are enhanced (or reduced). Respondents had purposes for their learning, but also gained purposes as an outcome of learning. Some of them talked about initial education as a time when their aspirations had been crushed. Others talked about how educational experiences (often in adult life) had helped them discover the direction they wanted to pursue.

The research found little evidence for a link between vocational or competence-based learning and mental health (or indeed social capital either). It seems that skills alone are not enough.

The recognition that possession of skills alone does not change lives, and that the process of individual and social change involves feelings, understanding and action is built into a national literacy assessment framework for the Irish National Adult Literacy Agency (NALA) (Merrifield, Coleman and McDonogh 2001; Merrifield, McDonogh and Coleman 2001). The NALA assessment framework sets out four main cornerstones of learning progress:

- knowledge and skills in the four areas of oral language, reading, writing and maths
- fluency and independence in literacy practices
- range of application of skills and knowledge (not just possession)
- depth of understanding and critical awareness.

I take from years of seeing learning change lives in many different ways some fairly simple lessons:

1  Learning does change lives but we cannot predict how, or plan for it. We only know it after the event.
2  Learners' own purposes for learning come directly from their hopes and aspirations, but also from things that happen in their lives. Whether that's having barrels of toxic chemicals float past their church to getting laid off from work, whether it's being forced by violence or economic necessity to migrate, whether it's children starting school or a separation, life provides an impetus for learning.
3  Literacy learning is as much a part of these purposes as any other, and little influenced by policy agendas that say people 'need' skills. The social practices view of literacy reflects that purposive, constructive approach and policies ought to be based on these concepts.

There is nothing new in this, but it is worth reminding ourselves that in the end, policies affect how we do things but mostly not why.

## Relationships between research, practice and policies

My own, fairly marginal, involvement with policymaking at the Center for Literacy Studies from 1988 to 1996 suggests that policy is seldom based on consistent, well-conducted and coherent research. I learned that the notion that research and policy are sequenced – the research gets done, the policy is based on it – does not happen much. I learned that some research is ignored and makes no difference at all to policy, some gets a lot of attention but makes no difference to policy and some (other people's research, not mine) does seem to get translated into policy. Policymakers tend to be selective, choosing what research to pay attention to (whether deliberately selective or out of ignorance of the rest does not really matter). A social practices study of policymaking would be interesting: what do policymakers read, how do they find it, how are they influenced by what they read (among all the other influences)?

My policy-related work at CLS addressed particularly performance and accountability issues. It culminated in a research report for NCSALL (the US national literacy research centre) called *Contested Ground: Performance Accountability in Adult Basic Education* (Merrifield 1998). What do we mean by performance, are we agreed on what good performance looks like, and does the field have the capacity to perform? Who is accountable to whom, how do we accommodate accountability to learners with accountability to policymakers and funders, and does the field have the capacity to be accountable?

The report was based on my experience as part of a project developing an interagency performance management system in Tennessee, research from the business world and interviews and group discussions with practitioners, researchers and policymakers in the field of adult literacy (all within the USA). *Contested Ground* had four recommendations to make performance accountability more democratic and more effective:

- *Agree on performances* – this is not a technical question but one of values, and the agreement on performance has to include the full diversity of purposes for literacy learning.
- *Develop relationships of mutual accountability* – in which one-way, top-down lines of accountability are translated into a mutual web of accountability relationships that involve different stakeholders (learners, teachers, managers, policymakers as well as taxpayers).
- *Build capacity to perform and to be accountable* – different kinds of capacity are needed but the two are linked through the learning organization approach in which ongoing information on performance and learner engagement helps programmes improve.
- *Create new tools to measure performance* – existing performance assessment tools are substitutes for the ultimate goals (whether these be more skilled and efficient workers, more active citizens or more involved parents) and are usually poor substitutes at that. We need new tools, and better understandings of what the tools are good for.

Embedded within these ideas, it now seems to me, is the necessity for the worlds of practice, research and policy to be intertwined for any of them to work well. Information on how well we are doing is as central for practitioners as for policymakers – practitioners need to develop research skills in order to improve what they are doing. Research is sometimes contradictory and inconclusive – policymakers need to understand the potential but also the limitations of research evidence. Research needs to start from the purposes of learners, practitioners and funders – researchers need a more responsive agenda and to work to make sure the research is understood.

We have spent some time in this seminar series bemoaning the fact that policymakers are so hard to pull into this kind of activity. I have spent a lot of time over the years thinking about practitioners' 'voice' and how to get it heard. Both are perfectly valid concerns. But both make assumptions about the separateness of the worlds of practice, research and policy that don't quite fit the lived reality. My experiences in crossing borders leads to some conclusions:

1   We tend to assume that policy is made 'out there' by someone other than us. But policy happens at lots of levels: it's about who has roles of power and how decisions are made. There is policymaking of a kind within a classroom. Certainly there is within a programme. And often we practitioners find ways of being selective about policy handed down from above – literacy practitioners have always been good at subversion. We do have power.

2   We often assume that policy has gone through a process of careful planning and that it cannot easily be challenged. But what I know about the reality is that policymaking is always rushed, and often policymakers are less confident about what they are doing than they seem. Policymakers are not a monolithic bunch. Policymaking is often a contested process within government as well as outside, and some are looking for information, stories and studies to use to back up their side of the argument. We ought to be cultivating them.

3   We assume that policy is based on research and analysis, but often it is not – or the research is done later to back up a decision that has already been made. The social practices view of literacy has been good at talking to practitioners but not so good at coming to the attention of policymakers. We need to promote a worldview that sees literacy in a different way if we want policy to reflect this.

## Conclusion

There are always opportunities for crossing boundaries. There are cracks within the system, boundaries are more permeable than they look, everything is messier than the neat divisions of research, practice and policy would indicate. We can encourage conversations across the borders. Mixing up research, practice and policy is not only possible but vital if each of them is to fulfil their roles effectively and enable adult education to make a difference in the world.

## References

Bell, B., Gaventa, J. and Peters, J. (eds) (1990) *We Make the Road by Walking: Conversations on Education and Social Change by Myles Horton and Paulo Freire*. Philadelphia, PA: Temple University Press.

Merrifield, J. (1993) 'Putting scientists in their place: participatory research in environmental and occupational health' in Park, P., Brydon-Miller, M., Hall, B. and Jackson, T. (eds) *Voices of Change: Participatory Research in the United States and Canada*. Westport, CT: Bergin and Garvey.

Merrifield, J. (1998) *Contested Ground: Performance and Accountability in Adult Basic Education*. NCSALL Reports No. 1, Cambridge, MA: National Center for the Study of Adult Literacy and Learning, Harvard University.

Merrifield, J., Bingman, M.B., deMarrais, K. and Hemphill, D. (1997) *Life at the Margins: Literacy, Language and Technology in Everyday Life*. New York: Teachers' College Press.

Merrifield, J., Coleman, U. and McDonogh, O. (2001) *Issues and Opportunities in Assessment*. Dublin: National Adult Literacy Agency.

Merrifield, J., McDonogh, O. and Coleman, U. (2001) *Mapping the Learning Journey: NALA Assessment Framework for Adult Literacy and Numeracy*. Dublin: National Adult Literacy Agency.

Schuller, T., Preston, J., Hammond, C., Brasset-Grundy, A. and Bynner, J. (2004) *The Benefits of Learning: The Impact of Education on Health, Family Life and Social Capital*. London: RoutledgeFalmer.

Street, B. (2001) 'Contexts for literacy work: the "new orders" and the "new literacy studies"' in Crowther, J., Hamilton, M. and Tett, L. (eds) *Powerful Literacies*. Leicester: NIACE.

# 15 Exploring Possibilities in the Boundaries

*Mary Norton*

With an area of 66,190 square km, Alberta is more than twice the size of the UK, and yet has less than 2 percent of the UK population. In 2004 the province's population was 3,124,923 (2004 official population list). Two-thirds of Albertans live in cities, with the rest living in villages or towns, on Metis settlements or First Nation reserves, or in places in between. The wide open spaces for which Alberta is known and loved also pose challenges for providing adult literacy and learning opportunities.

I have lived in Alberta since 1973, at first in a northeastern town that had been a fur-trading post in the 1700s, and since 1977 in Edmonton, the provincial capital. I was drawn into adult literacy work in the late 1970s through my first career as a public librarian, and in 1980 I was hired as a literacy consultant in the Alberta government. My consultant role included supporting the development of community-based literacy projects, encouraging coordination among various sectors that provided literacy programmes, and doing some groundwork related to policy development.

My practice as a government consultant was influenced by my connections with the field and my continuing academic education. In 1985 I left the consultant's position and enrolled in a graduate programme, focusing on adult literacy.

Since 1992 I have worked at The Learning Centre, a community-

based adult literacy and education programme. Although I identify most strongly with my role as coordinator and facilitator at the Centre, I continue to cross boundaries as I engage in literacy research in practice and in consultations related to policy development.

In this chapter, I consider some possibilities and challenges for applying social practices perspectives to literacy programming under current provincial and federal government policies. In particular I explore how people might be supported to practice and develop literacies through expanded 'points of access' (Hamilton 2000) within a perspective of lifewide learning. I start with an overview of literacy policy/provision in Canada and Alberta, noting that both are under review.[1]

## Policies for literacy provision

In Canada, delivery of adult literacy education, along with basic and post-secondary education, is the responsibility of the provincial and territorial governments. In Alberta, the Department of Advanced Education and the Department of Human Resources and Employment share this responsibility.

Federally, the National Literacy Secretariat, through its national literacy programme, works in partnership with provincial and territorial governments and with non-government, business and labour organizations to promote literacy. The NLS supports and funds activities that include the development of learning materials, promotion and public awareness efforts, and applied literacy research. (National Literacy Secretariat – Key Activities 2005).

Federally and in Alberta, literacy is promoted as a means for people to participate more fully in 'lifelong learning, work and citizenship so they are able to contribute to a democratic, knowledge-based and prosperous society' (Alberta Learning[2] 2004: 2). To this end, Alberta Advanced Education provides for delivery of literacy and adult basic education through post-secondary institutions and through community-based programmes. For the most part, ABE programmes in the post-

---

[1] In 2005 the Minister of Alberta Advanced Education initiated a consultation process to set directions for advanced education in Alberta, including adult literacy education (*A learning Alberta: Framing the challenge* 2005). Also in 2005 the government of Canada made a commitment to work with partners, including the provinces and territories, to develop a strategy to support the development of literacy and essential skills.

[2] In 2004 Alberta Learning was divided into Alberta Advanced Education and Alberta Education.

secondary sector are intended to prepare people for employment or for training/further education that would lead to employment.

The community adult learning programmes (CALP) policy (Community Adult Learning Program 2002) provides for community adult learning, ESL and literacy. Under this policy, Alberta Learning funds community adult learning councils (CALCs) and volunteer tutor adult literacy programmes (VTALPs). The CALCs coordinate and promote adult learning in a council area, and distribute grants to subsidize delivery of or directly deliver literacy, ESL, community issues and employability enhancement programmes. In most communities, the CALCs are responsible for the VTALPs.

The colleges are the major provider of adult basic education in Alberta, both in terms of budgets and numbers of participants. However, in this chapter I focus on the CALP policy because it relates to my work, and because of the possibilities it affords for offering and expanding access to literacies.[3]

## Applying social practices theory within community literacy programmes

The VTALPs provide one-to-one and small group tutoring by volunteers for adults to improve their 'functional literacy skills for further education, employment preparation or personal reasons' (Community Adult Learning Programs 2002: 23). In my experience, the Alberta policy reference to 'functional skills', along with a policy requirement to 'tailor instruction to individual learner's needs' (Community Adult Learning

---

[3] In 2004 there were 83 CALCs and 71 VTALPs in Alberta (outside of Edmonton and Calgary). In 2002–03, there were 4,012 literacy participants in CALC courses and 1,120 in VTALPs (Bradley Wells 2003).

Programs 2002: 23), encourages programming that *could* be shaped to reflect a social practices approach.

As Yvonne Hiller noted, 'the practice of teaching literacy reinforces the notion of social practice, but many practitioners would be unlikely to label their approach as a social practice approach' (Hillier 2004: 1). Similarly, 'social practices' is not part of the vocabulary of most practitioners in Alberta or Canada, although literacy researchers have worked within a social practices perspective for some time. Rather, the idea of 'teaching in context' has been widely promoted in the community-based literacy sector, and tutor and programme coordinator training has focused on teaching cognitive strategies for constructing meaning through interaction with relevant texts.

My own academic grounding in reading as a cognitive process has posed some challenges in crossing boundaries from teaching in context to applying social practice theory. For instance, in a peer-tutoring project (Norton 1997), I anticipated that tutors would model the cognitive strategies that I introduced in tutor training. Instead, they 'just' read! And in the course of reading – and talking and writing – both the learners and the peer tutors extended their practices:

> [A]fter writing about the rural one-room school of her child-hood, a student decided to research and write about 'School in the old days'. A peer tutor helped her read the books she had borrowed from the library and found himself getting caught up in 'learning the history of the old schools, going through it with her and reading the books myself, finding the way things were'. (Norton 1997: 10)

I continue to value and draw on my understanding of cognitive processes. However, I think that modelling and direct instruction in cognitive processes can be integrated with a social practices approach. Social learning, as I observed in the peer-tutoring project, also provides opportunities to cross boundaries between teaching in context and facilitating from a social practices perspective.

## Social learning

Guy Ewing argues that 'if literacy is a set of practices within a social network, a community, then it must be learned within a community' (Ewing 2003: 17). According to Ursula Howard, 'learning is part of "social being", drawing in the skills, ideas and knowledge of others' (Howard 2003: 4).

Creating contexts for drawing on the skills, ideas and knowledge of others could be seen as a challenge under the current Alberta policy for VTALPs, given the focus on one-to-one tutoring.[4] Although learning with a volunteer tutor involves more than one person, learning in groups, or in a setting where it is possible to interact with other people, extends the opportunities for social learning.

The CALP policy does provide for volunteer tutors to work with small groups. However, small populations, vast service areas and diversity of learners' interests pose challenges for organizing groups in some rural areas. Even where it is possible to form groups, current VTALPs funding may not be used to pay tutors or hire instructors. Instructors or facilitators can be hired under the community adult learning council policy, but in rural areas VTALPs tend to be the main approach to adult literacy provision.

In urban settings, VTALPs are often one of various approaches, both across programmes, and within a programme. As an example, The Learning Centre involves volunteer tutors but also receives funding from the CALC to hire facilitators for literacy and community issues programming. This means that people who attend the centre may choose to participate in one or more ways: with a tutor, with a group, on their own, or in a project. Some participants also tutor others.

## Power

Social learning can lead to a shift in relationships between tutors/ facilitators and learners and provide opportunities for sharing power. Working from a social practices perspective intersects with power relations in other ways as well.

Certain literacy practices, such as the practices of schools and other institutions, are privileged over others (Hillier 2004). In the Alberta community-based context, whether the more privileged practices are presented as the 'correct' ones, or as avenues for expanding choices, depends more on the experiences and beliefs of tutors and learners, than it does on policy requirements. The extent to which a tutor and learner 'unpack' the social context of, for example, correspondence from an institution, also depends on experience and stance, as well as on the learner's interests and needs.

---

[4] As well as helping adults to acquire literacy skills, VTALPs are seen as a way to 'mobilize volunteer resources to support learning' (Community Adult Learning Program 2002: 23).

As well as examining the contexts of texts, social practices approaches encourage people to examine and reflect on the contexts of their lives, with a view to taking action for change (Tett 2003). As an example, a group of women at The Learning Centre undertook a project to research resources and services for people in literacy programmes. As they identified resources, some women told about leaving abusive relationships and one woman's story led to another. The group posed questions, such as 'Why do women stay in an abusive relationship?' and pooled their knowledge to come up with answers. They talked with counsellors and visited shelters to find out about available resources for women living with experiences of violence. Eventually the women developed a script which they presented to participants, tutors and staff in other programmes and agencies. Their presentation raised awareness about experiences of violence and how they affect learning, and provided opportunities for the women to speak and be heard.

Speaking and being heard – having a voice – has been identified as a valued outcome for learners in literacy programmes. In some VTALPs, serving on boards and committees or participating in learner support groups provide context for developing voice, as well as for having a say in programme operations. Recently, a group of adults from Edmonton literacy programmes formed a group called Students Voices for Students. The group meets to share information, support each other, develop confidence and self-esteem and to speak out about literacy. They have made some public presentations about literacy and hope to present to various community agencies and organizations.

## Assessment

It is important that learners, tutors and facilitators have opportunities to take stock of progress and reflect on how their learning and teaching is going. The community adult learning programmes policy requires that programmes 'demonstrate progress towards the learner's goals' (Community Adult Learning Program 2002: 23).

Social practice theory opens avenues for participatory assessment that starts with people's practices and interests. Through a 'reflective learning' project at the Centre, we experimented with various approaches to working with learners to document learning and were challenged to find ways to help participants articulate how they were applying their learning in their lives outside the centre. A further challenge is to report on learning in ways that answer policy needs.

The IALS results have been used widely in Canada to promote literacy. However, the IALS is based in an understanding of literacy that may be at odds with a social practices account of literacies and with the nature of teaching and learning in literacy programmes. In her analysis of the IALS study, Susan Sussman noted that:

> What gets said about literacy in public awareness campaigns ... may be highly relevant to literacy rate statistics but not entirely relevant to what goes on in literacy programs, which tend to be shaped by realities and needs of learners and practitioners. Many of the important gains made in literacy programs may never show up in literacy rate statistics. We run the risk of winning public and political support today because of what the numbers show, only to lose it tomorrow because of what the numbers don't show. (Sussman 2003: 8)

A federal House of Commons Standing Committee consultation about literacy heard that 'setting goals and establishing accountability mechanisms are critical components of a successful approach for raising low literacy levels' (*Raising Adult Literacy Skills: The Need for a Pan-Canadian Response* 2003: 14). Notions of 'evidence-based education' are also being discussed and introduced in Canada. In some cases, evidence-based research values the findings of scientific research and the use of random assignment experiments (Comings 2003). Others advocate that 'evidence' can be gathered by a range of methods. The House of Commons Standing Committee encouraged 'as broad a consultation as possible with literacy stakeholders to identify goals and performance measures' (p. 15).

These developments present opportunities – and related challenges – to develop assessment processes that relate to learners' practices *and* address policy needs.

## Participation

A study of rural VTALPs programmes (Bradley Wells Management Consulting 2003) identified a decline in participation in literacy programmes in some rural communities and suggested a province-wide initiative to promote literacy and a lifelong learning culture. Activities to promote literacy may serve adults who see a need and value in enrolling in programmes. However, in a study of patterns of participation in literacy programmes, Ellen Long and Sandy Middleton (2001) noted that people with low literacy skills are aware that social, economic and political forces besides literacy levels shape their lives. Juliet Merrifield (2004) noted that 'people may exclude themselves from an education system that seems alien, unfamiliar, and with no value in the social context they inhabit' (Merrifield 2004: 1). According to Alan Quigley (1997), people may actively reject programmes that seem like a school based on middle-class values. This does not mean, however, that they do not value learning and education.

The Bradley Wells report also noted a difference in coordinators' and individuals' perceptions of literacy needs: 'Coordinators identify individuals who have low literacy level as needing service. However, these individuals may not perceive a need to improve their literacy skills. They may be content with their quality of life, have well paying jobs and/or function well generally in the community' (Bradley Wells Management Consulting 2003: 31).

Differences in perceptions pose challenges for engaging adults in literacy programmes. However, when considered within a social practices view, they also point to possibilities for expanding access – possibilities that could come to fruition under current CALP policy.

## Expanding access/integrating literacy and lifewide learning

The Bradley Wells report identified limitations of the volunteer tutor model and suggested a 'more flexible approach, where tutors and paid staff work side by side, technology enables some self-direction, both classes and individual instruction are available, and literacy services are closely linked to other services in the community including k-12, post-secondary, health, employment and social services systems' (Bradley Wells Management Consulting 2003: 33).

I agree with the suggestion for a more flexible approach for literacy provision that could increase possibilities for applying social practices theory and may draw in more people. Still, I think that literacy programmes, however organized, are often associated with 'school' in one way or another and as such will appeal to some people, sometimes. Literacy programmes have a role in 'direct delivery' but they can also be catalysts for expanding points of access (Hamilton 2000) for literacies, within an understanding of lifewide learning that recognizes the range of formal, non-formal and informal settings in which people learn, the range of people who facilitate learning, and the range of ways in which learning may be demonstrated.

Recent research in Canada has explored how adults with little formal education learn. Through interviews with adults, Niks et al. (2003) found that although reading is a common learning strategy, adults also learn by asking, observing others, and 'just doing it'. Wright and Taylor (2004) found that adults involved in literacy programmes also engage in a range of 'informal learning' outside the programmes.

In a literacy needs assessment by the Communication Energy and Paperworkers Union (2004), those surveyed reported that they had learned skills in such settings as sports team coaching, union work and leading a youth group such as scouts. In a review of community contexts for women's learning, Hayes (2001) identifies a 'vast and rich array' of organizations and groups. All of these could be points of access.

The Connecting Literacy to Communities project (Gardner 2004), funded by the National Literacy Secretariat, offers a model for expanding points of access by integrating literacy awareness and development into community settings. Initiated by Bow Valley College in Calgary, the project grew out of an identified need to expand adult literacy programmes at the community level and the need to increase awareness among service providers about ways to make their programmes and services more accessible for people with limited literacy.

Taking a research in practice approach, the project was carried out over two years in three rural and three urban communities. It built on theory and practice in the areas of community development, community capacity building, *literacy as social practice* and facilitating organizational and social change. One of the questions that guided the project was: in what different ways do people use literacy in their everyday lives?

Literacy 'specialists' were contracted to work with agencies in health, social services and education fields, and in some cases, with private businesses. Among other work, the literacy specialists formed partnerships with agencies, to explore ways to make agency services more literacy friendly, to create adult literacy initiatives within organizations, and to provide professional development for staff about literacy access. Examples of initiatives include a computer class in a library, a GED course in an adult literacy programme, and a Scrabble group in a seniors' residence. Follow-up to the project has included workshops and an online course to introduce the concepts to coordinators of community-based literacy programmes across the province.

For me, writing this chapter was one catalyst to develop a three-year 'widening access to adult literacies' project, which was initiated in autumn, 2005.[5] Through a partnership between The Learning Centre and a community-based social services agency, the project intends to

---

[5] The Widening Access for Adult Literacies Project is funded by the National Literacy Secretariat, Human Resources and Skills Development Canada, in partnership with the Community Adult Learning branch of Alberta Advanced Education.

address issues of participation by planning, implementing and assessing approaches to widen access to literacies. Approaches include integrating support for literacies development into existing community programmes and services, offering 'taster' courses to invite adults into learning, and offering informal courses that support intentional literacies development. Using community development and participatory education approaches, the project will draw from and build on research and practice about literacies, participation, reducing barriers, and creating supportive environments for learning. I am excited about the possibilities this project offers for the local community and for learning more about how to apply social practices perspectives.

## Conclusion

Ursula Howard (2003) suggested that 'policy can encourage and prioritize – it cannot actually prevent or control', and that 'change and development also happen regardless of policy'. Yvonne Hillier (2004) reported on the 'debate on whether our response to policy should be through subterfuge and subversion, through creativity or through challenge'. Yvonne also raised the question, 'How are we going to use the opportunity of the policy moment which is so focused currently on basic skills?'

In this chapter, I have discussed how it is possible to apply a social practices approach within a particular policy framework. The framework is not explicitly based on social practices theory, however, and coordinators, tutors and learners do not necessarily teach and learn from a social practices perspective – just as my practice is not always consistent with social practices theory. Opportunities to learn and reflect about social practices could be one way to clarify assumptions about literacy/literacies, encourage reflection, and push the boundaries of policy and practice.

It is also important to have opportunities to learn and reflect critically about IALS and the more recent ALLS, about policy statements, about funding[6] and the focus on volunteers, and about the ways in which literacy and education does and does not make a difference for people and communities. Although the Alberta population is among the most highly educated in Canada, and although the province is enjoying

---

[6] Grants to rural VTALPs average $25,000 per year. Funding to VTALPs outside Edmonton and Calgary totalled $1.8 million (Bradley Wells Management Consulting 2003).

an economic boom, child poverty, homelessness and the use of foodbanks continues. Addressing these and other issues of social inequity require an education of the heart, as well as an education for the mind.[7]

# References

Alberta Learning (2004) '2004–2007 business plan'. Edmonton, AB: Alberta Learning. Also downloadable from www.learning.gov.ab.ca (accessed 5 April 2005).

Alberta Municipal Affairs (2004) 'Official population list', downloadable from www.municipalaffairs.gov.ab.ca/ms/pdf/2004pop.pdf (accessed 2 October 2005).

*A learning Alberta: Framing the challenge* (2005) 'Review of the advanced learning system', downloadable from www.advancededucation.gov. ab.ca/alearningalberta/ (accessed 10 October 2005).

Bradley Wells Management Consulting (2003) *Review of Basic Literacy and English as a Second Language in Alberta's Smaller Communities*. Edmonton: Community Adult Learning Programs Branch, Alberta Learning.

Comings, J.P. (2003) *Establishing an Evidence-based Adult Basic Education System*. NCSALL Occasional Paper. Cambridge, MA: National Centre for the Study of Adult Learning and Literacy. Also downloadable from ncsall.gse.harvard.edu/research/op_comings3.pdf (accessed 10 October 2005).

Communication Energy and Paperworkers Unions of Canada (2004) '*Literacy learning needs assessment*', downloadable from www.nald.ca/ fulltext/cepuc/p1.htm (accessed 10 October 2005).

Community Adult Learning Program (2002) *Policy and Operating Requirements*. Edmonton, AB: Alberta Learning.

Ewing, G. (2003) 'The new literacy studies. A point of contact between literacy research and literacy work'. *Literacies*, 1: 15–19.

Gardner, A. (2004) *Building Community Capacity: Focus on Adult Literacy*. Unpublished report.

Hamilton, M. (2000) 'Sustainable literacies and the ecology of lifelong learning', downloadable from www.open.ac.uk/lifelong-learning/ papers/393CCAC1-000B-67AA-0000015700000157.html (accessed 10 October 2005).

---

[7] In a forum in Vancouver, the Dalai Lama, Archbishop Desmond Tutu and Iranian law professor Shiran Ebaldi spoke about the need for education that stresses compassion as well as technological advance (Todd 2004).

Hayes, E. (2001) 'Social contexts' in Hayes, E. and Flannery, D.D. *Women as Learners. The Significance of Gender in Adult Learning*. San Francisco: Jossey Bass.

Hillier, Y. (2003) 'Reflections on the May 16th seminar' ESRC Adult Basic Education Seminar Series, downloadable from www.education.ed. ac.uk/hce/ABE-seminars/papers/Seminar3-Reflections.pdf (accessed 10 October 2005).

Hillier, Y. (2004) 'Crossing boundaries or boundary crossing. From practice to research and research to practice.' Unpublished paper prepared for the ESRC Adult Basic Education Seminar Series, downloadable from www.education.ed.ac.uk/hce/ABE-seminars/papers/ABE6-YvonneHillier-Research.pdf (accessed 10 October 2005).

Howard, U. (2003) 'How could a socio-cultural approach to literacy, numeracy and ESOL inform policy?' Unpublished paper prepared for the ESRC Adult Basic Education Seminar Series, downloadable from www.education.ed.ac.uk/hce/ABE-seminars/papers/ABE1-Ursula Howard.pdf (accessed 10 October 2005).

Long, E. and Middleton, S. (2001) 'Patterns of participation in Canadian literacy programs: results of a national follow-up study' in Taylor, M.E. (ed.) *Adult Literacy Now*. Toronto, ON: Culture Concepts.

Merrifield, J. (2004) 'Questions arising from Lynn Tett's paper on social exclusion' ESRC Adult Basic Education Seminar Series, downloadable from www.education.ed.ac.uk/hce/ABE-seminars/papers/ABE6-JulietMerrifield.pdf (accessed 10 October 2005).

National Literacy Secretariat (2005) 'Key activities', downloadable from www.hrsdc.gc.ca/en/hip/lld/nls/About/keyactiv.shtml (accessed 10 October 2005).

Niks, M., Allen, L., Davis, P., McRae, D. and Nonsuch, K. (2003) *Dancing in the Dark. How do Adults with Little Formal Education Learn? How do Practitioners do Collaborative Research?* Duncan, BC: Malaspina University College.

Norton, M. (1997) *Getting Our Own Education. Peer Tutoring and Participatory Education in an Adult Literacy Centre*. Edmonton, AB: The Learning Centre Literacy Association.

Quigley, A. (1997) *Rethinking Adult Literacy Education. The Critical Need for Practice-based Change*. San Francisco: Jossey Bass.

Report of the Standing Committee on Human Resources Development and the Status of Persons with Disabilities (2003) *Raising Adult Literacy Skills: The Need for a Pan-Canadian Response*. Ottawa, ON: House of Commons.

Sussman, S. (2003) *Moving the Markers. New Perspectives on Adult Literacy Rates in Canada*. Ottawa, ON: Movement for Canadian Literacy.

Tett, L. (2003) 'ABE and social inclusion'. Unpublished paper prepared for the ESRC Adult Basic Education Seminar Series, downloadable from www.education.ed.ac.uk/hce/ABE-seminars/papers/ABE3-LynTett.pdf (accessed 10 October 2005).

Todd, D. (2004) 'Schools urged to teach ethics'. *Edmonton Journal*, April: A5.

Wright, B. and Taylor, M. (2004) *Purposeful Literacies through Informal Learning. A Resource for Literacy Practitioners*. Ottawa, ON: Partnerships in Learning.

Women of Courage (2003) Unpublished presentation.

# 16 Crossing Boundaries or Boundary Crossings: From Practice to Research and Research to Practice

*Yvonne Hillier*

## Back to the beginning

Throughout this book, we have debated how numerous contexts relate to a social practice view of language, literacy and numeracy. Many of these chapters have drawn on our seminar series conducted between October 2002 and May 2004. In Chapter 1, we 'set out the stall' about a social practice view of ALNL. Is it possible to identify at what point we can cross from practice to research by examining more deeply what we mean by a social practice view? Can we test whether the social practice view is something that can be understood through research?

The practice of teaching literacy, numeracy and language is through the *deliberate* use of literacy events. Those of us who have taught either literacy and numeracy, or both, will recognize the types of activities that we use to reinforce the acquisition of the functional and skills aspect of literacy and numeracy, such as writing a note for the milkman or teacher at school, reading a bus timetable and so on, rather than acquiring the basic rules of grammar or computational skills. So the *practice* of teaching ALNL reinforces the notion of a social practice, but many practitioners would be unlikely to label their approach as a social practice approach. For them, it is common sense to teach basic skills through the use of everyday situations. Yet the type of work that is undertaken in basic skills sessions across the country is often deemed to be functionalist, because it is dealing with the kinds of skill necessary to operate, for example, function, in the workplace and in the home.

Is there a clear distinction between the social practice approach and the functional literacies approach? The latter is used to enable people to *manage* their lives, often with an emphasis on being able to cope in the workplace or with families. It recognizes the status quo of any situation. The challenging consequence of a social practice approach is that it recognizes the power dimension in literacy, where institutions demand practices which confer status and material goods. Schools and uni-versities require certain uses of literacy, numeracy and language, and if these are not demonstrated, people may not study at these institutions and cannot gain degrees that lead to work which often has a higher remuneration than for people without such qualifications. Awarding bodies provide qualifications that demonstrate that individuals have gained the ability to apply specific uses of literacy, numeracy and language. Even being able to write a letter of complaint, or assert a grievance verbally with confidence ensures that some individuals are privileged compared with those who cannot do these things. The use of high levels of mathematical skills enables many young people entering the labour market to command higher salaries than those who have difficulty with the use of maths and or have no qualifications in this subject. The current debate about qualifications, stimulated by the Tomlinson Report (2005), is evidence that different uses of literacy are recognized by the government and employers. Functional literacy and numeracy is apparently privileged by employers, even though the academic 'gold standard' of A levels (and highers in Scotland) is used as a screening tool which separates those who can write using a variety of registers from those who have just mastered the 'basics' of reading, writing and numeracy. Thus one difference between a social practice and a functionalist approach is that the former recognizes where there are inequalities which are maintained through uses of ALNL, and attempts to challenge the 'proxies' for privilege, whereas the functionalist approach merely helps people work within the structures. It is a small step, then, to arguing that the social practices approach is more appropriate, and even more desirable than a functionalist approach, because ultimately it will be more enabling for adults.

## Challenging the taken for granted

If we assert the desirability of a social practice view of ALNL, how does it affect the everyday practices that occur? Are we merely describing these everyday events in a particular way? What difference can it make? In other words, can we undertake research into our claims by trying out the social practice approach and identify what happens as a result? I have realized that in order to understand such practices, we need to stop repeating what we do simply because this is how we were trained to do it, or because it seemed the best idea at the time. An example of how to begin an examination of these 'taken for granted' approaches is through looking at our own biographies as practitioners. I would like to share my own faltering steps to recognizing that I took things for granted and where self-doubt crept in to such an extent that I began doing something about it.

Originally a volunteer, part-time tutor and then an organizer from the late 1970s until the early 1990s, my growing experience in a basic education scheme was supported and developed through numerous half-day and full-day training days offered regionally, funded by the Adult Literacy and Basic Skills Unit (ALBSU). When I first became an organizer, the parting words from the outgoing organizer were: 'There's a volunteer training course starting in four weeks. You will see what I have done in the file but I am sure you know what to do.' And that became the trigger for my first journey into research. The thing was, I was not sure I *did* know what to do. I had experienced, first hand, two volunteer training programmes in London and Birmingham. I read the ALBSU newsletters, and attended the training events. We talked all the time about good practice. I managed to bluff my way through running my first volunteer training programme and distinctly remember mentioning good practice throughout each session. Who was I to assume that my version of good practice was the 'right one'? More fundamentally, did I know what good practice was?

During this time, I had begun first a master's degree, and then, still hankering after academic knowledge, a doctorate. I still had this unsettling thought that I did not know what good practice really was and that other people, 'out there' possessed this knowledge. Occasionally, people do have the 'aha' moment, when they realize that there is a link between two ideas which are discussed in completely different disciplines, or they can see their way to answering a question that has been challenging them. I was fortunate, in the late 1980s, to have such a moment, when I realized that I could apply my original knowledge of psychology, to this question about good practice. I had been reading a book by Usher and Bryant (1989) called *Adult Education as Theory, Practice and Research: The Captive Triangle* in which the authors claim that much of our practice is informed by theory that we do not easily articulate. In other words, we use tacit or implicit knowledge to guide our practice. I realized that this tacit knowledge was what I needed to capture in order to find out what good practice was. Usher and Bryant could not offer a way to elicit this tacit knowledge, and this is where my hazy psychology memories began to stir. There is a theory of how people make sense of their world, called personal construct theory, created by George Kelly (1955). He had developed a technique, called the repertory grid, which could elicit people's ways of construing the world. And so began my first 'proper' research into basic skills. I subsequently published the results, thus entering a new world of academic writing (Hillier 1998). And this is where crossing the boundary from practice to research begins. Many people spend their time thinking about their practice and indeed, they often try out small research activities even though they might not label these activities as research. To really make research into practice explicit and available for others to read about and try out, research has to be disseminated in some way. For most practitioners, writing about their own practice, and particularly about any small-scale research into their practice, is not something that they would normally think to do. There are journals in which practitioners can publish their work, for example, in the *RaPAL Bulletin* and *Adults Learning*. These publications have a wide readership, and probably are highly influential, but I doubt that anyone has ever tried to establish the effect of these publications on people's practice. Only when people do cross the boundary from practice to research do they begin to enter the real possibility for sharing their findings and more importantly, critically examining them. As the practitioner researchers in Tomlin (this volume) show it is not easy to move from being a practitioner to a researcher, and it is particularly difficult to influence a wider audience.

## Critical reflection

When I eventually came to City University to run a master's programme for people who were involved in the education and training of adults, my research journey became even more focused. The master's programme was underpinned by the notion of reflective practice. I had come to realize that to develop practice required making explicit the tacit, and therefore unchallenged, assumptions about what we do. I had also developed an understanding of the need for testing our assumptions and of course we can only do that if we have made them explicit in the first place. These ideas stemmed from a number of theories that I had begun to examine. Most influential was Stephen Brookfield (see for example, 1993, 1995) who writes so eloquently about challenging our assumptions and the much earlier work by John Dewey (1933). Both writers exhort us to take a step outside our everyday practice: 'One can think reflectively only when one is willing to endure suspense and to undergo the trouble of searching ... to be genuinely thoughtful, we must be willing to sustain and protract that state of doubt which is the stimulus to thorough enquiry' (Dewey 1933: 176).

Neither writer suggests this is an easy thing to do, but until we 'hunt' our assumptions, we cannot fully demonstrate why our actions are justified.

I have written before about the challenges of being critically reflective (Hillier 2002). If we do think about our practice and try to challenge our beliefs in a positive way, we will be able to search for new understandings of our practice. We can then 'take control over our practice, acknowledging that we cannot transform everything, but aware that we can identify the spheres in which we can. It is a truly emancipatory process' (Hillier 2002: 25).

It is all very well *thinking* reflectively, but without doing anything as a result, we continue to practise as before. How do we know that our newly challenged assumptions are going to make any difference to what we do? More pressingly, how can we take action and identify whether this is effective? To do this, we need to undertake action research.

## Taking action

If we return for a moment to the claims made by the social practice approach, we can see that we can now define how we should act in certain ways. For example, Lyn Tett suggested that a social practices view of literacy and numeracy, set within a social justice context would require that literacy and numeracy is organized within contexts that integrate feelings and values among the more common focus on skills (Tett 2003: 5) and, in this volume, Tett further suggests that 'learning programmes that are grounded in life situations can encourage participation by responding to issues that are derived from people's own interests, knowledge, expertise and experience of the world. This is much more likely to encourage learning that has a value to those that use it'.

This would suggest that we might wish to change the way in which we address our approaches to teaching and learning (or more likely, acknowledge that we do this despite it not being a part of the national curriculum!). However, to be truly challenging of what we do, we must test out our ideas of a social practice approach. Action research does not only consist of people's reflections on what they *have* done. It is research while action *is taking place*. It is a deliberate attempt to 'examine the way in which something is being undertaken, with a view to making changes to that process as the research goes along. It is therefore a more fluid, and iterative process than evaluation of past practice. It is self-critical and is located in an approach that aims to develop practice through systematic enquiry. It has a 'fundamental and explicit aim to make a difference' (Hillier and Jameson 2003: 57).

## Identifying claims

What are the claims of a social practice approach that we should begin to research in this way? The research agenda has been clearly set by practitioners who have asked a number of important and challenging questions in the seminar series (see www.education.ed.ac.uk.hce/ABE-seminars/index.html):

- How do we integrate a social practices approach into provision if we are to improve social inclusion?
- How do we listen to the voices of our learners, rather than 'giving them a voice'?
- What are the challenges for practitioners in the implementation of the 'alternative' social practice approaches?

Previous chapters have offered answers to these questions. Thus, when we consider social inclusion, Ursula Howard has argued people do not learn best as isolated individuals; that they learn interactively. She suggests socio-cultural approaches, for example, situated literacies, are about an inclusive view of people's lives. Lyn Tett has contextualized how a social practice approach to ALNL can begin to tackle social exclusion: '[W]hile learning alone certainly cannot abolish the deep-rooted causes of social exclusion it can make a useful contribution to combating it, not least by tackling the ways in which social exclusion is reinforced through the very processes and outcomes of some types of literacy and numeracy education' (Tett this volume).

This can be done if a curriculum is developed that helps students to recognize that they have the capacity to learn and to generate new knowledge that will be really useful to them. This can be achieved by developing the awareness of employers, policymakers and other decision-makers about the value of using a social practices, rather than a deficit, approach to literacy and numeracy (Tett 2003: 5–6).

For language learners, Celia Roberts advocates that learners need to be able to understand the behaviours, values and practices of a community in order to use language (Roberts 2003). However we need to recognize that in the classroom, they do not define themselves as 'immigrant' or 'newcomers'. There are therefore tensions to be managed, not least because learners are categorized for example as EFL or ESOL learners, which relates to the ethnographic notion of 'insider/outsider'. Elsa Roberts Auerbach concludes that we need to undertake research to help 'uncover the patterns and points of tension experienced in people's lives which can then become content for the curriculum' (Roberts Auerbach 2003: 4).

In this volume, Elsa suggests that social practices research can enable learners to act on their own behalf to challenge inequities and change conditions of their lives, but that this social practices research has to be a particular variety to effect such change.

What does a social practices view do to give learners their voice? One thing it can do is move beyond the idea that difficulties are 'not just to do with people's failings, issues of debt, or needing help with a form'. Instead, David Barton suggests that people's understanding of literacy is an important aspect of their learning, and that people's theories guide their actions (Barton this volume). The social practices view, then, is more concerned about what people can *do*. It offers a 'richer' description that can identify many more potential points for intervention or leverage in efforts to facilitate literacy development. It can provide an integrated framework in which the provision of basic skills programmes can itself be understood as a set of literacy practices (Reder 2002).

The trend so far, that we can discern from the claims made in this book, is that a social practices approach is one which will help learners be more proactive in their worlds, and which will help prevent policymakers and managers thinking of people who need to improve their basic skills as having *something wrong*, being worse off than someone else who has no such problems, in other words, a challenge to the deficit model of basic skills. What can this mean for practice? Again, our authors have provided a number of claims and assertions which are testable.

There are some more pragmatic claims that are ideal research topics. For example, Diana Coben asserts that 'seeing through to the maths' in a situation is crucial. Once people see that there is something mathematical to be done which produces a way through a problem, they may find the actual mathematics relatively straightforward (Coben this volume). However, Diana recognizes that most people do not 'speak mathematics as a first language' and they need to be taught it. Indeed, as Tomlin, Baker and Street (2000) argue many 'numeracy events' are invisible to people, and therefore the parallel with the social practices approach to literacy is not so clear cut.

There is not room to discuss how we can undertake the research to elucidate the claims outlined above, but where it does take place, these claims and challenges can, as the quest for evidence in policymaking continues, provide support for, and an opportunity to change, policy and practice. Our book has attempted to address the way in which a social practice of literacy can be applied to a number of contexts (Barton this volume; Barton and Hamilton 1998). Within this notion, is an implicit assumption that the social practice of ALNL is 'a good thing' and that more functional approaches are 'a necessary thing'. Furthermore, the functional approach has taken precedence over the former due to the influence of government policymaking and the drive for meeting targets, particularly in England. In contrast, Scotland has developed a more community-based approach to basic skills, where the targets involve measures of participation rather than numbers gaining qualifications. The debates about the impact that government policy is having on our practice hold many claims about the deleterious effects (see Derrick and Lavender this volume), but once again, if we start 'hunting' our assumptions, we may begin to find that we have little evidence that practice has been truly changed by such policies. A more unsettling thought is that we do not know how effective a social practice of literacy approach is. This is particularly hard to challenge, as a social practice approach, by its very nature, attempts to validate the everyday practices of working with words, numbers and language. How can we challenge such ingrained and *normal* activities?

## Communities of practice

Given that a social practice approach to ALNE includes the practices of teachers, researchers and policymakers, we can begin to see that we belong to a number of communities of practice. Lave and Wenger (1991) argued that we join a community and learn more about it and how to behave within it through 'legitimate peripheral participation'. Our knowledge of how our community functions is established through our developing sense of identify. If we, as practitioners, become involved in research into our practice, we join another community, that of researchers. If we also wish to influence policymaking, we may join yet another community. It is the same for our learners, who join a different community when they undertake formal learning activities, and we know how many of them feel initially out of place because they have a view about what such a community is like, until they try it out. There is, of course, a wonderful opportunity to influence the community one joins, by bringing practices from elsewhere to shape and influence the emerging practice. I suggest this is where we need to expend our energies.

## Crossing boundaries

The original boundary crossed from practice to research has to be *crossed back* to practice from research. Indeed, rather than thinking of going back to practice, it is better to think of crossing *forward*, taking the notion of critical reflection and action research to enable us to inform our practice. Many of us today are painfully aware of the need to challenge policy initiatives that are steering our practice along paths which we may not wish to tread. Yet a truly reflective approach will cause us to challenge not just the new policies, but also our own stance. This is particularly uncomfortable.

Crossing the boundary requires places where we can cross. Some are easier than others. To continue the metaphor of a journey, it is much easier to ford a stream with a bridge than by wading through. It is easier to cross from practice to research, because there are set ways or bridges that have been set up. We can enrol on postgraduate programmes and learn how to undertake small-scale research. Once we have acquired some research experience, we can continue to make inroads into our knowledge by reading about other research with a more informed understanding of what is being said, and because we can undertake more research ourselves. I think it is far harder to cross from research to practice, because of the tendency to follow the 'high road' of academic research, rather than to keep both feet on the ground and, therefore, get them dirty. The trouble with getting our feet dirty is that it is uncomfortable, often unglamorous and there are few opportunities to rise above and claim what we are finding.

So where does this leave the boundary between research and practice? I do not think we have closed borders with guards protecting the passage into their protected territory. I do think we have traffic flowing more in one direction than the other. I also suggest that we have to continue to force ourselves to move into the spaces where we feel uncomfortable, where we know we do not have the answers, and where we even have to question the ideas we do hold dear. It is by questioning, and finding a rationale for what we do, that we become strong and able to provide evidence that supports our actions. I think this is the challenge, and the path we need to take if we are to influence the other boundary crossings between research, practice and policy.

# References

Agar, M. (1994) *Language Shock*. New York: William Morrow.

Barton, D. (2002) 'A social practice view of language, literacy and numeracy.' ESRC Adult Basic Education Seminar Paper, downloadable from www.education.ed.ac.uk.hce/ABE-seminars/index.html (accessed July 2005).

Barton, D. and Hamilton, M. (1998) *Local Literacies: Reading and Writing in the Community*. London: Routledge.

Brookfield, S.D. (1993) 'Breaking the code: engaging practitioners in critical analysis of adult education literature'. *Studies in the Education of Adults*, 25(1): 64–11.

Brookfield, S.D. (1995) *Becoming Critically Reflective Teachers*. San Francisco: Jossey Bass.

Coben, D. (2003) 'Adult numeracy policy?', downloadable at www. education.ed.ac.uk.hce/ABE-seminars/index.html.

Dewey, J. (1933) *How We think: A Restatement of the Relation of Reflective Thinking in the Educative Process*. Chicago, IL: Henry Regenery.

Hillier, Y. (1998) 'Informal practitioner theory: eliciting the implicit'. *Studies in the Education of Adults*, 30(1): 35–53.

Hillier, Y. (2002) *Reflective Teaching in Further and Adult Education*. London: Continuum.

Hillier, Y. and Jameson, J. (2003) *Empowering Researchers in Further Education*. Stoke-on-Trent: Trentham.

Howard, U. (2002) 'How could a socio-cultural approach to literacy, numeracy and ESOL inform policy?', downloadable from www. education.ed.ac.uk.hce/ABE-seminars/index.html (accessed July 2005).

Kelly, G. (1955) *The Psychology of Personal Constructs: Vols 1 and 2*. New York: Norton.

Lave, J. and Wenger, E. (1991) *Situated Learning: Legitimate Peripheral Participation*. New York: Cambridge University Press.

Reder, S. (2002) 'Notes as discussant Seminar 1 October', downloadable from www.education.ed.ac.uk.hce/ABE-seminars/index.html (accessed July 2005).

Roberts Auerbach, E. (2003) 'Aligning social practices research with critical approaches', downloadable from www.education.ed.ac. uk.hce/ABE-seminars/index.html (accessed July 2005).

Roberts, C. (2003) 'Language, literacy and bilingualism: connecting theory, policy and practice', downloadable from www.education.ed. ac.uk.hce/ABE-seminars/index.html (accessed July 2005).

Tett, L. (2003) 'ABE and social inclusion', downloadable from www. education.ed.ac.uk.hce/ABE-seminars/index.html. (accessed July 2005).

Usher, R. and Bryant, I. (1989) *Adult Education as Theory, Practice and Research: The Captive Triangle*. London: Routledge.

# Index

# DIMENSIONS OF ADULT LEARNING
## Adult Education and Training in a Global Era

## Griff Foley (ed).

"Griff Foley has done those of us who are interested in adult learning a favour ... Dimensions of Adult Learning provides an up-to-date, internationally relevant and comprehensive overview of an increasingly diverse field of study ... an ideal introduction to the field for teachers, researchers and policy-makers."
Journal of Education and Work

"[The book] lives up to its ambitious name and has something to offer policy-makers and practitioners who want to take a fresh look at the expanding world of adult learning."
Talisman

"This timely and valuable book makes an important contribution to our understanding of key recent developments in adult education and their significance. Reflecting the increasingly global nature of scholarship in the field, well-respected international contributors analyse issues facing practitioners today and consider how these can be most positively embraced to further the international cause of adult learning and social justice."
Janet Hannah, University of Nottingham.

This broad introduction to adult and post-compulsory education offers an overview of the field for students, adult educators and workplace trainers. The book establishes an analytical framework to emphasise the nature of learning and agency of learners; examines the core knowledge and skills that adult educators need; discusses policy, research and history of adult education, and surveys innovations and issues in adult education and learning. It also examines adult learning in different contexts: on-line learning, problem-based learning, organisational and vocational learning.

Edited by internationally known academic Griff Foley, the book features chapters from leading contributors in the UK, North America, Australia and worldwide.

**Contributors:** Damon Anderson, Francesca Beddie; Carmel Borg; Bob Boughton; Mike Brown; Shauna Butterwick; Tara Fenwick; Laurie Field; Keith Forrester; Vernon Galloway; Andrew Gonczi; Nancy Grudens-Schuck; Joce Jesson; Linda Leach; Peter Mayo; John McIntyre; Paul McTigue; Mike Newman; Tom Nesbit; Kjell Rubenson; Peter Rushbrook; Tom Sork; Barbara Sparks; Bruce Spencer; Peter Stephenson; Nelly Stromquist; Lucy Taksa; Mark Tennant; Shirley Walters; Michael Welton
352pp

0 335 214487 (EAN: 9 780335 214488) Paperback
Not for sale in Australia, New Zealand or Asia

# ADULTS LEARNING
## Fourth edition

## Jenny Rogers

*"... many teachers of adults would improve their teaching by rigorously following the advice and structures outlined in this book."*
International Journal of Lifelong Education

This friendly and practical book is *the* guide to how to teach adults. It builds confidence, offers practical advice and gives the real-life flavour of the privilege and excitement of helping fellow adults develop. Now in its fourth edition, the book has been extensively rewritten to meet the needs of those working with adults at the beginning of the 21st century.

- The book answers questions such as:
- How do adults really learn?
- How can I put over my material in a way that will interest and excite people?
- How can I manage my group so that the confident people don't dominate and the quieter ones get a look in?

*Adults Learning* is for anyone who wants to know how to teach adults in a wide range of settings – from traditional adult education institutes, universities, management training courses to government training schemes.

**Contents:** Introduction / Adults learning: what you need to know / Giving feedback / Understanding your group / Teaching mixed ability groups / The first session / Lectures and demonstrations / Case studies, role play, simulation and games / Discussion and facilitation / Tutoring open learners / Coaching and mentoring / Evaluating learning / Bibliography / Index.

240pp 0 335 20677 8 (EAN: 9 780335 206773) Paperback

# TEACHING ADULTS
## Third edition

## Alan Rogers

In the 3rd edition of this bestselling text, Alan Rogers draws upon a range of recent work on adult lifelong learning to address this key question, by looking at what is distinctive about adult learning and teaching. Based on nearly 40 years of practical experience in a variety of contexts in the UK and overseas, the book discusses what it is that makes helping adults to learn different from teaching younger students. It is concerned with both basic principles and useful hints for teachers and, as such, it is of value to teachers and programme organisers, students on adult education courses, policy makers, and administrators. The emphasis throughout is on the practice of teaching through greater understanding of what it is that we are doing – and the author speaks with involvement and from experience.

The third edition provides a comprehensive handbook for students and practitioners with important insights into contemporary understandings of how adults learn both formally and informally, and how they can be helped to learn. Its overall theme – that of making the natural and largely subconscious learning which all adults do both more conscious and more effective – resonates with current thinking and has received much support from the growth of interest in adult learning outside formal learning situations. An invaluable resource for lecturers and trainers, this book will also appeal to those such as health visitors and clergy who are primarily engaged in other activities.

**Contents:** Preface and acknowledgements / Introduction / Before you start / A contract to learn / Definitions / Adult students / The nature of learning / Learning and teaching / Pause for thought / Goals and objectives / Adult learning groups / Roles and the teacher / Teaching: content and methods / Pause for more thought / Blocks to learning / Evaluation / Participation / Conclusion / Bibliography / Index.

304pp    0 335 21099 6 (EAN: 9 780335 210992) Paperback